Media and Popular Musi

Media Topics

Series editor: Valerie Alia

Titles in the series include:

Visit the Media Topics website at www.euppublishing.com/series/MTOP

Media and Popular Music

Peter Mills

EDINBURGH
University Press

© Peter Mills, 2012

Edinburgh University Press Ltd
22 George Square, Edinburgh

www.euppublishing.com

Typeset in 10/12 Janson Text
by Servis Filmsetting Ltd, Stockport, Cheshire, and
printed and bound in Great Britain by
CPI Group (UK) Ltd, Croydon, CR0 4YY

A CIP record for this book is available from the British Library

ISBN 978 0 7486 2749 3 (hardback)
ISBN 978 0 7486 2751 6 (paperback)
ISBN 978 0 7486 3156 8 (webready PDF)
ISBN 978 0 7486 6444 3 (epub)
ISBN 978 0 7486 6443 6 (Amazon ebook)

Contents

Acknowledgements

I'd like to thank everyone who has been kind enough to speak to me in the preparation of this book:

James Addyman, Laura Barton, Simon Broughton, Mark Cooper, Mark Ellen, Jeremy Lascelles, the Rusby family, Jane Siberry, Fiona Talkington, Ben Watt and Paul Williams.

Thanks to Helen Wilson at *The Guardian* for permission to reproduce Laura Barton's work.

Thanks to Valerie Alia and the staff at Edinburgh University Press for their patience and support.

Glossary

ABC figures   Magazine sales figures for the UK.

Borrowed interest   The 'value' which is accrued by a product from an association with a well-known song or a famous person via endorsement or advertising.

Cultural gatekeeper   A person or organisation which exerts control over whether works are seen or heard by a wider public or not, and mediate between those artworks and their potential audience, guiding their audience toward or away from that work. They are often trusted by their audience to make such judgements – Melvyn Bragg is a good example from popular culture.

Jingle   A short, specifically composed song designed to function as part of an advert for a given product. Coca-Cola has a very long history of commissioning and employing jingles.

Metatext   A text which is about more than itself, and goes beyond what it speaks of – in popular music, a song like 'My Way' is a good example of a metatext.

RAJAR figures   Radio listening figures for the UK.

Introduction

In this book, we examine key ways in which media and popular music intersect and help each other do business. When Van Morrison said 'Music is spiritual; the music business isn't' he was merely replying briefly to a journalist's question but in doing so identified a central issue for any study of music and the way it is marketed, distributed and mediated. Television, for example, is born to be sold, no matter how aesthetically pleasing or expertly made it may be. Likewise, film exists because there is a demand for movies. Music, however, does not depend on its economic value in order to exist – it may well depend on commercial 'realities' to remain in the marketplace or to form part of the narrative arc of a career, but music has a primal connection to human experience. It existed long before ways were devised to sell it.

The relationship between music and the processes via which it is mediated set it apart from other media forms with which it is routinely grouped. We explore, via a number of case studies, the ways in which creativity is brought to the marketplace – how the deep human urge towards music meets the demands of industrial economics (Bourdieu 1987: 6). The book covers the mediations of popular music on British television and radio, and in a range of publications from daily newspapers to specialist magazines; it also looks at the role of the independent label in keeping the roots of music developing and how such labels mediate that music. These categories allow us to explore the role of the cultural gatekeeper in constructing the way that music and musicians are understood by their actual and potential audiences. We do this by talking to professionals who work in the industry.

The growth of Popular Music Studies since the late 1960s reflects the development of the form post-1945 and the willingness of the generation who grew up listening to pop to take it seriously. That mix of the serious and the frivolous is key to the soul of popular music of any form, genre or culture – it is something fit for love and dancing but also has the power to move, galvanise and disseminate ideas within a society via the unstoppable force of the remembered song.

1

A link between music and its social power is not confined to a single generation. Thanks to the changing technological mediations of music, the post-Second World War generation could access music and musicians in ways that were previously impossible. For example, on 9 February 1964, more than 73 million people simultaneously watched the Beatles on *The Ed Sullivan Show*. Likewise, recording technologies make it possible for us to listen to Enrico Caruso or Frank Sinatra, Nick Drake or Kurt Cobain any time we like, though all have long since departed. Through such examples, this book explores how popular music is mediated in practice. It places professional and artistic practice in a new theoretical framework.

Music does not exist separately or in isolation from the society or culture that produces it. So while considering how music is mediated by TV, radio and print we also acknowledge that these elements are connected. We might assume that cultural production is, in Wernick's phrase (Wernick 1991), 'promotional culture' but surely the mediation of popular music is also doing something else – it enables the music to endure beyond the moment of its performance. Recording technologies have allowed the 'capture' of the momentary and made it permanent. This has changed the dynamics of the human relationship with music and our own creativity. Thus the secret of music's significance in contemporary culture lies in the mediating technologies which catch, record and recreate the unique moment. This applies equally to the pages filled with writing *about* music.

Indeed writing about popular music is something of an enigma; perhaps even more than writing on film or television, it produces all kinds of writing in different registers, tailored to address different readers. Some say it is impossible: polymath Martin Mull infamously likened writing about music to 'dancing about architecture' and 1960s countercultural icon Frank Zappa described music journalism as being 'written by people who can't write for people who can't read'. Others say it is essential. We shall consider both viewpoints.

Writing about music falls broadly into one of two categories: on one side consumer writing, scholarly and academic on the other. The former is assumed to focus upon personalities and ephemera, including fan writing and coverage in mainstream newsprint. Writing in the specialist music press (titles like *Q* or *NME*) feels less engaged in promotion yet is in its own way just as closely allied to the processes of the music industry, built to promote and sell product. Scholarly work on popular music tends to set aside the ephemeral and concerns itself with the canon, focusing upon artists and works the cultural value of which has passed beyond mere 'taste' and 'opinion' and is effectively a cultural norm. There is consensus in both fields about the value of, say, the Beatles, Bob Dylan or the Sex Pistols but the differences lie in the manner in which they are written about. These recordings still sound the same as they did when newly issued; it is the way in which they are discussed which has changed. Thus what remains to be explored in writing about music is the way in which such works can be shown to be exceptional: this is the role of the cultural gatekeeper (see Becker 1992; Hesmondhalgh 2007) as much as the technological mediator.

It's true to say that writing about popular music has been distinguished from – and kept at some remove from – traditional musicology, or writing about classical or 'serious' music. To some extent these boundaries are breaking down as rock and pop develops a canon of high cultural value – the Beatles or the blues – while classical music is marketed more aggressively to a younger, wider audience. This process began with violinist Nigel Kennedy in the 1990s and is currently best embodied by 'pop-opera' singers such as Welsh singer Katherine Jenkins and Paul Potts who was discovered on ITV's *Britain's Got Talent* show. Likewise, artists such as 1960s band the Kinks and 1980s act Madness are seen as equally expressive of 'Englishness' as the work of classical composers such as Sir Edward Elgar (1857–1934) or Ralph Vaughan-Williams (1872–1958). The renowned music scholar Richard Middleton considered the ways popular music is understood by musicologists, noting that 'there is a rich vocabulary for certain areas [he cites harmony, tonality, certain part-writing and forms], which are important in musicology's typical corpus' yet there is 'an impoverished vocabulary for other areas, such as rhythm, pitch, nuance and gradation, and timbre, which are less well developed' (Middleton 1990: 104–6).

In the same way that much of the rock and pop catalogue is, directly or indirectly, influenced by the work of the once-obscure 1930s bluesman Robert Johnson (see Guralnick 1998; Wald 2005), it is undoubtedly the case that all scholarly writing about popular music is indebted to Theodor Adorno's essay 'On Popular Music' (see Leppert 2002). Adorno was part of the famous 'Frankfurt School' of thinkers (see Bottomore 2002) and the essay was written in 1941 after the German Jewish intellectual had arrived in New York after fleeing Nazi persecution in his homeland. It shudders with the shock of the new, describing the impact of jazz and big band music – that is the popular music of 1941 – upon his senses, after he had left the Europe of Beethoven and Wagner. After Adorno, there were isolated examples of early writing about popular song in socio-cultural terms, in works such as Richard Hoggart's *The Uses of Literacy* (1957) and a prescient piece on the Beatles by a young Terry Eagleton (1964), but effectively it took scholars nearly three decades to catch up with Adorno's thoughts on the nature of popular music.

The subject, and the search for a new descriptive vocabulary, arguably began in earnest through the free journalism of the late 1960s in magazines like *Rolling Stone* and *Creem* in the USA and *Time Out* and *Oz* in the UK, which then fed into in the early work of writers like Greil Marcus and Lester Bangs in the US. Marcus's *Mystery Train* (1972) is rightly a standard work of pop criticism and his professionalism contrasts starkly with the wilder stylings of Bangs, a more intuitive writer but preyed upon by his own weaknesses for drink and narcotics; his work is gathered in several anthologies such as *Psychotic Reactions and Carburetor Dung* (2001). Marcus is currently a professor at Berkeley in California; Lester Bangs died of an accidental drug overdose in April 1982.

In the UK the innovators included Richard Middleton and Simon Frith, who both began to write about pop in British publications in the early 1970s. Middleton could be argued to be the 'father' of Popular Music Studies, introducing the subject to serious study and founding the influential journal *Popular Music*. Middleton is a musicologist who argues for the presence of a dedicated field of popular music studies to be accommodated within the wider field of musicology. This has been explored and argued in works including *Pop Music and the Blues: A Study of the Relationship and Its Significance* (1972), *Studying Popular Music* (1990) and a collection of work from *Popular Music* published as *Voicing the Popular: On the Subjects of Popular Music* (2006). As a sociologist Simon Frith has tended to look at popular music and its ebbs and flows as sociological phenomena as much as artistic or aesthetic creativity. Books like *Sound Effects* (originally published as *The Sociology of Rock*, 1978), *Performing Rites* and *Music for Pleasure* (both 1998) have all worked away at this particular seam to illuminating effect. Key works by subsequent scholars include Bennett (2000, 2001), Hesmondhalgh (2002, 2004), Inglis (2003, 2006), Moore (2009), Negus (1996, 1999), Shuker (2001, 2007), and Whiteley (1993, 2000, 2005); all have made a substantial contribution to the teaching of the subject in the UK while American scholars such as Grossberg (1992) and Reising (2002, 2006) have set the topic in a wider context of public life within a consumer culture. Major monographs on the work of major artists such as the Beatles (see Macdonald 1994), Bob Dylan (see Shelton 1986/2011), Van Morrison (see Mills 2010) and Marvin Gaye (see Ritz 2005) have all expanded the popular music studies bookshelf. Surveying the field, we note how frequently key texts have been edited collections – where there are many voices addressing the topic (see Inglis 2010), or 'users guides' which aim to act as primers for study (see Shuker 2007, revised 2011). Both are useful approaches; the ensemble effort of the edited volume is somehow appropriate to the socialised and socialising power of popular song.

Structure and logic

Each section has an introductory essay which considers the specific field and its history as well as considering the key theories which have been influential upon the subject. This is followed by the case studies which seek to test the theory against the actual experience of those who write about, broadcast and make the music.

The first part of the book is arranged through studies of three key media forms to which music finds itself subject: press, television and radio. First, we look at mainstream rock and pop magazine publishing with Mark Ellen, who has been at the forefront of this field since the late 1970s and whose professional biography is effectively a history of UK music magazine publishing, taking in editorships at *Smash Hits*, *Q*, *Select*, *Mojo* and *Word* magazines. His insights are illuminating and generous. Following this we consider how popular music finds its way into a daily newspaper through a discussion with Laura Barton, music writer for *The Guardian* and author of the highly regarded 'Hail, Hail, Rock'n'Roll' column; there is a sample edition of this column in the book's Appendix I. Specialist or 'niche' magazine publishing is explored via a discussion with Simon Broughton, editor of the 'World Music' magazine, *Songlines*. Finally we look at an odd one out – a magazine for the trade. Where the previous three writers have been involved in consumer publications, *Music Week* is the trade paper for the British music industry and as editor Paul Williams observes, it is 'the village paper' for the business. This presents us with a different model of the mediation of music and we consider how this reversed polarity changes the way music is thought of and understood in this specific context, alongside a case study of a single issue of the paper.

Where consumers can choose to read or not to read the printed word, it might seem that music on television is harder to escape – after all MTV licensed a sample from Kraftwerk's 1986 track 'Musique Non Stop' to promise (or threaten) exactly that – music, non-stop. Yet as satellite channels delivered music and pictures around the clock, popular music coverage on terrestrial television became much rarer. Content in contemporary British television, for example, is either historical-contextual documentary such as seen on BBC4 or, in rare oases, live performance such as the BBC's coverage of the Glastonbury festival. Since BBC1's *Top of the Pops* was cancelled in 2006 the idea of the competitive chart has disappeared as a structural device for presenting popular music on British television. This has democratised much of the visual mediation of pop but has arguably taken some of the pleasurable heat and light out of the process. Mark Cooper has produced the BBC's flagship music show *Later . . . with Jools Holland* for twenty years and through his expertise we consider the role of television in the mediation of popular music.

With equally illuminating observation, Jeremy Lascelles, CEO at music and media company Chrysalis, discusses the relationship between music and advertising. What is being 'sold' here? Music, product, or both? 'Borrowed interest' seems to be part of the connection between music and advertising, but we discover that it is not the whole story. His choice examples, from cult hero Nick Drake to electro dance act Leftfield, come from his extensive experience in the industry and make for an eye-opening exploration of this topic.

Finally we examine two BBC specialist music shows, one for national broadcast and one for local. BBC Radio 3's *Late Junction* provides a model for how an individual original idea can influence the directions in which the mediation of music can head and also how those same mediations can impact upon individual musical reputations; the show's first and longest-term presenter Fiona Talkington offers a range of insights into the nature of music radio and what it takes to get a piece of music on the air. The second case study is a show produced for BBC Radio Leeds, *Down in the Grooves*. Host and originator James Addyman discusses how and why a show like this is able to get on air, become successful and then maintain that success despite being moved around the schedules and occupying an unpromising timeslot. This leads to a consideration of whether, with the advent of 'Listen Again' platforms such as the BBC iPlayer, the concepts of 'national' and 'local' radio broadcasting are breaking down. The powerful streak of originality of ambition and purpose which runs through these two radio shows links us into the second part of the book.

In the book's final chapter we examine, through two case studies, the nature of independent musical production and mediation. The subjects of these studies, 'Pure Records' and 'Buzzin' Fly', are excellent examples of both the struggles and successes experienced by labels which stand outside the commercial mainstream yet which are very successful in both commercial and creative senses. How do they 'manage' such success without outgrowing their own roots and sense of identity with which each is strongly identified? Pure is the home of

English folk singer Kate Rusby, and is a very successful independent label, with sales figures and balance sheets which would be the envy of many mainstream companies. That the label has remained effectively a family-run operation while managing great commercial success is most remarkable and the discussion with the Rusby family reveals much about the difficulties as well as the rewards of running a label in this way.

Buzzin' Fly operates in another 'niche' market, that of dance music, and as such is obliged to deal with many of the economic realities that face a label like Pure even though their musical catalogues could hardly be more diverse. The label's founder, Ben Watt, best known as half of the band Everything but the Girl, discusses how the label began and how the day-to-day realities of running a label according to aesthetic as well as economic criteria can impact upon the way the music is made, distributed and understood. We also learn how a label might expand into other media forms, such as 'branded' club nights and radio programming. Both examples represent a faith in the wider meaning of music as an art form which can exist for other reasons than just to be sold and embody a resolution to maintain some genuine independence in a marketplace which seeks to force creativity into the centre ground. In their mediations, then, they are seeking to foreground the music itself, for itself. In the space between such level-headed business sense and the creative forces which drive music lies a fascinating tension. This book seeks to explore that tension between creativity and industrial process, and how music survives its multiple mediations.

1 Dancing about Architecture? Mediating Popular Music Through the Written Word

Introduction

The music press in the UK is long-established and yet essentially modern (see Gorman 2001; Jones 2002). It needs to be connected to the historical contexts of the music it discusses, with all the connoisseurship and 'gatekeeping' this implies, but also needs to reflect what is happening now, today, and furthermore to spot the trends of tomorrow. It is required to perform a kind of balancing act, holding these elements together. The old weekly titles, with their remarkable turnover of copy and subject matter, dealt with this directly: who was in, who was out. These magazines functioned more as an information exchange than a consumer guide and this is a key difference between the newsprint weeklies of the past and the monthly glossy magazines which, since the advent of the compact disc in the mid-1980s, have replaced them.

The oldest music weekly in the world, the *Melody Maker*, was founded in London in 1926, as a paper for working musicians, a kind of trade paper. It kept this function until well into the 1980s, with the rear section of the paper given over to 'classifieds' where bands looking for players or players looking for bands would advertise. This set it apart from the other weeklies in the period after the arrival of the Beatles which were chiefly consumer or 'fan' publications while the *Melody Maker* was the paper read by musicians, the people who actually played as opposed to simply listened – the producers rather than the consumers. The paper was published without interruption, even surviving the London Blitz, recording the musical life of the country even in the deepest days of the Second World War (1939–45). At first the paper included scores, competing with the established sheet music business, and developed the idea of popular song as being a subject worthy of critical scrutiny, effectively inventing the idea of music journalism. It had been in print for over twenty-five years before *New Musical Express* (note the claim on novelty in its very title) was even published, and the eclectic mix of jazz, folk, blues, country, classical and rock and roll all treated equivocally continued until it closed in 2000.

To meet the demand for pop writing, the *Musical Express and Accordion Weekly* had been bought by music promoter Maurice Kinn in 1952. Renamed *New Musical Express* (*NME*) from November 1952 it followed the example of the leading American music publication *Billboard* by publishing charts, initially of sheet music sales. This was the first time such figures had been made public in Britain. The paper thrived, according to Kinn, precisely because of this new, competitive dimension which it added to the marketplace – the chart changed the way people looked at pop and it snapped into clear focus the new postwar dynamic between art and the market. In acknowledgement of this *Melody Maker* felt obliged to introduce its own chart in 1958.

The new world of the pop star and the chart rundown drove a burst of highly coloured magazine titles: *Record Mirror*, launched in 1953 by Isidore Green, embraced the new conditions even more rapidly than the *NME*, being the first weekly to assume the reader as non-musician and furthermore to be as interested in the lives and preferences of the performers as the music. It became a respected if more lightweight companion to the *NME*, the 'poppiest' of the weeklies, with the distinction of being the first national to publish an article on the Beatles. Another weekly, *Disc*, arrived in 1958, catching the waves of the 1960s and 1970s before eventually being absorbed into *Record Mirror* in 1975, which itself disappeared in 1991 by which time the musical and publishing landscapes had changed completely.

It was the arrival of the Monkees on television in late 1966 that really opened up the music press, making a divide between the pop and rock papers which has never really been restored – suddenly there was music for kids and music for more sophisticated readers/listeners. The writing about the music inevitably reflected this. So for the fans of this new serious or 'heavy' music, a weekly called *Sounds* was launched in October 1970 by United Newspapers. This was expressly targeted at the new, proven to be literate audience who had made American magazines like *Rolling Stone* (1967–), *Creem* (1969–89) and *Who Put the Bomp* (1970–9) a success even at import prices. Never as left-field as the *NME* but more fan-based than the *Melody Maker*, *Sounds* shadowed the musical policies of the period closely, not unlike that of the BBC's 'heavy' television programme, the *Old Grey Whistle Test* (see Mills in Inglis 2010), favouring American boogie bands of the early 1970s, then jumping on board punk quite quickly, then latterly talking up the 'New Wave of British Heavy Metal', a sort of heavy Britpop which gave us Def Leppard, Iron Maiden, Girlschool and others. The magazine also unwisely got involved with the Oi! Punk offshoot in the early 1980s and never really recovered its reputation before being shut down in April 1991. Tellingly, the most enduring and successful spawn of *Sounds* was *Kerrangg!* magazine, a monthly niche title launched in 1981 by Bauer Media, targeted at the most loyal readers of *Sounds*, the heavy metal fans – the title of the magazine being an onomatopoeic invention, suggesting the sound of a highly amplified guitar chord of the type favoured by heavy rock players. *Kerrangg!* is now a global brand and franchise, alongside various media outlets on television and radio.

It was not until 1986 that a mainstream rock and pop monthly arrived. *Q* magazine opened the floodgates for similar titles, all monthly magazines (*Vox*, *Select*, *Mojo*), which quickly became the dominant force in the marketplace for mediating popular music in print. Unlike the weeklies, which had focused firmly on this week's news and events, the monthlies had the whole of music history to work with, and were well placed to present CD reissues as 'rediscoveries'. The idea of a magazine that covered only what was happening this week became anachronistic, especially since the daily press was by now taking such an interest in pop. The successful monthlies combined humour and authority. This mix was partly borrowed from superior fanzines such as *Zigzag* (1969–86) which trumped the weeklies and led the way between the post-1960s comedown and the arrival of punk: such specialism survives in luxurious niche publications such as *Shindig!* (2007–).

However, what really changed the landscape of music journalism in the UK was the arrival in 1978 of a glossy fortnightly magazine called *Smash Hits*; it successfully drew together disparate and even tribal musical forms by simply presenting them as what was fashionable and successful at that particular moment – in this its model was not unlike that of *Top of the Pops*, the BBC's most famous music television show which would simply present what was popular each week regardless of genre. I spoke to Mark Ellen, the magazine's most well-regarded and influential editor about his views on the business of writing about music.

The mainstream pop and rock magazine editor – Mark Ellen of *Word* magazine

The narrative arc of Mark Ellen's career is effectively that of the post-punk British music magazine publishing industry. He began writing pieces for *Record Mirror* (1954–91), the *NME* (1952–present) and London listings magazine *Time Out* (1968–present) before

joining *Smash Hits* (1978–2006) in 1983. He went on to found *Q*
(1986–present), *Select* (1990–2000), *Mojo* (1993–present) and *Word*
(2003–present) magazines, effectively indexing the growing-old of the
original audience for writing about popular music in the UK. This
was in addition to a stint of presenting the *Old Grey Whistle Test* for
BBC2 between 1984 and 1987, including being one of the presenters
for the BBC's *Live Aid* coverage on 13 July 1985. I spoke to him about
his work and how he saw the role of the music magazine as mediator
of pop.

> *PM:*   I'm interested in the lineage of the British pop magazine
> from *Smash Hits* to the *Word.*
>
> *ME:*   Well I've been involved in all of those, so it's a personal
> lineage, I'm not sure whether they're part of the same family tree
> . . . they might be, I'm not sure, I've never really thought about
> that! Certainly there are people who started out reading *Smash
> Hits* when they were 12 or so, when I was working for it in the
> early 80s, then graduated to *Q* magazine, *Select*, *Mojo* and maybe
> *Word* now . . . I know this because people write and tell me! So I
> suppose people seem to like a certain sensibility about the things
> I've been involved with, which obviously must be something to
> do with my character coming through . . . [laughs] . . . they like
> the general feeling of the magazines, some kind of warmth or
> humour that they connect with.

So here we see how, while the magazines were reflective of the
musical output and 'product' of their time, the magazine was a kind
of creative space in which responses to that 'product' could be shaped,
played with, even manipulated. This has much to do with the nature
of the approach to that task – Mark Ellen coins it as 'a warmth and
humour' which comes through, and which exists as a kind of line of
continuity running through the various titles and their responses to
their subject, be that a one-hit wonder like Plastic Bertrand or the
Beatles' *White Album*. We spoke about how his connection to this
lineage started out:

> *PM:*   I remember my sister buying a magazine called *Disco 45*,
> which simply contained the lyrics to current pop songs and
> *Smash Hits* had a bit of that, didn't it?
>
> *ME:*   Well *Smash Hits* was launched off the back of the success of
> *Disco 45* by a man called Nick Logan who had worked at the *New
> Musical Express* and had left the *NME* and was about to start *The*

Face from some offices off Carnaby Street, and the idea was to go into that pop market which he saw as a major, burgeoning area, off the back of disco really: the Bee Gees, Olivia Newton John, and all those disco songs that were such a great success in the 70s. You realised that there was an appetite for people wanting the actual song words, as there was no way of getting them . . . you couldn't 'Google' the lyrics, and it seemed like a very important accompaniment to the single, if you were 12 or 13 and a girl probably – it was felt to be a girl's market really – he used that idea as the basic structure for the launch of *Smash Hits*.

So *Smash Hits* had its roots in the sense of such a magazine being a kind of mediator between an audience and the product – building on *Disco 45*'s utilitarian provision of song lyrics and capitalising upon shifts in mediation and the flow of information about individual songs and artists.

ME: What happened was *SH* did incredibly well, it got lots of advertising, and it was able to expand in its pagination. However, we kept the number of lyrics the same and developed the amount of editorial, that was just humorous, interviews, reviews and observations and just created this whole club, really, for teenagers who were obsessed with buying pop singles and watching *Top of the Pops*. It was really aimed at people who weren't old enough to go out . . . I always had this theory about it, it was like an electrical circuit, which started with the buying of the record, and then hearing the record on the radio and maybe watching the group on *TOTP*, and all you needed to link up the circuit was the printed lyrics, a poster or an interview . . . an encounter with the person making the record, and those were the three things we supplied to the circuit, and that's what would turn the magic fairy lights on! It seemed to work . . . but a lot of the success of *SH* was that it had a rather psychedelic sense of humour I think. It looked at the pop landscape as being like a huge cartoon, and it managed to exaggerate the characteristics of the people who were the main players in that picture, so Morrissey was important, this English eccentric with a hearing aid and NHS glasses and gladioli stuffed into his back pocket, or Madness, these boys with their little cars . . . Simon Le Bon was this bulky character with a tea-towel swept across his face! We played them up into being these characters . . . which worked for and against the artists' view of themselves of course, but let the readers in a bit.

Smash Hits succeeded by acknowledging the new appetite for information about the personalities both of and behind the pop product. This it did by deliberately injecting humour into the process – this is something which the *NME* and *Sounds* had done at the margins, but only occasionally allowed into the actual text, when it could be a blunt instrument – as Chris Salewicz and Charles Shaar Murray recalled (Gorman 2001: 183), Bryan Ferry in particular became a target for the *NME* – all this being an offshoot of the 'new journalism' which came in on the coat-tails of punk. Prior to this, the press as a rule took its subject very seriously – this is why the earnest interviews with bands like Uriah Heep from 1973 in the weeklies now seem so arcane. This barbed humour was a development of certain aspects characteristic of writers like Nick Kent and Charles Shaar Murray pre-punk, and borrowings from the Lester Bangs school of music writing on publications like *Creem*. All of this still retained the sense that the journalist was 'superior' to the reader – a cultural gatekeeper's role in effect – but the difference *Smash Hits* made was to bring the audience on board with the in-jokes – as Mark Ellen said, it 'let the readers in a bit'.

Clearly the sense of a readership in on the joke and belonging to a community was central to the magazine's success – the escapist nature of pop, directly codified by the music and presentation of bands like Adam and the Ants, was echoed in the playful fantasies and high silliness spooled out in the pages of *Smash Hits*. This represented a dramatic shift in tone for the mainstream British music press, away from the seriousness of the monochromatic weeklies and into the brilliant candy-colours of the early 1980s scene, with videos and TV at the centre. Mark Ellen recalled such differences as being ones of temper as well as tone:

> PM: The weeklies, such as the *NME* and the *Melody Maker*, were built to do a different job . . . the psychedelic, brightly coloured humour of *SH* was refreshing in comparison and yet the two complemented each other very well. Do you think the style of *SH* as you've been describing it actually changed the way pop music was written about, in the British press at least?
>
> ME: Well that's a really good point . . . I think maybe it did, for a number of reasons. One was that it wasn't judgemental in the way the weeklies were because obviously it was aimed at a much younger audience, and I felt personally very strongly that you didn't want to put all that in there necessarily . . . I'd come from *NME* when I was about 23 or 24, so I was surrounded by people writing 8,000 word articles about Devo, the overture to which

before they met the band in Los Angeles would be 4,000 words of conjecture and cant about themselves or their ridiculously ill-informed views on the city . . . stuff that had nothing to do with the group at all! Now obviously that was a different readership but I felt that you should remove those obstacles and try and connect the people reading it as immediately as possible with the subject. They wanted to read about Madness, or Culture Club, they didn't want us getting in the way, really. Another thing was that the magazine was quite funny and also very affectionate, it sent them [the acts] up and allowed them to send themselves up, and I think that was quite refreshing. So the weeklies were very 'grey' in content as well as look, printed in black and white while *SH* was printed in colour on good quality paper, so that was a fantastically revolutionary thing because the music that we wrote about only existed in colour, I think. The New Romantics in particular was a colour concept . . . a black and white picture of Spandau Ballet or Culture Club was meaningless! So to return to your question I think it did change things because *SH* also influenced the language a lot, not only in how musicians could be described but it started to invent its own language for its readers . . . idiosyncratic spellings and names for people, Simon Duran and the like, so that the act and the person became indivisible but very lightly so.

Ellen suggests that the combination of humour and colour both reflected and created a strong sense of identity among the audience who followed these acts and, thereby, increased awareness of and emphasis on such aspects of representation within promotional mediation for the acts themselves – so if a black-and-white picture of Culture Club or Spandau Ballet was 'meaningless', in what way was meaning created? Ironically, Spandau Ballet's roots were in the New Romantic or 'Futurist' club scene, in places like 'Blitz' in Covent Garden, 'Heaven' at Charing Cross and later in the 'Rum Runner' in Birmingham and the 'Warehouse' and 'Le Phonographique' clubs in Leeds where the monochromatic, high-intensity shadows and over-tones of Weimar German decadence were a very important part of 'the look' and the attendant self-mediation – club-going as theatre. Here, black and white was most 'meaningful' indeed. However, by the time the 'faces' of this scene such as Boy George, Steve Strange and, more briefly, Marilyn were in *Smash Hits* as fully-fledged popstars the 'colour splash' was key. The colour harmonised with the new medium of the promotional video which, even in the pre-MTV landscape, was fast becoming the dominant promotional tool and which could make a substantial difference to the fortunes of a song and an act. Likewise, a group like Madness captured lightning in a bottle by matching their onstage personae perfectly to the new media – Madness existed as 'characters' both in and out of their videos, record sleeves and magazine interviews. This issue of intention and attitude is pertinent to the journalists themselves of course – they may have occasionally written like smirking teens but as Ellen confessed:

> *ME*:　The thing was that at *SH* we were all over-qualified. We'd all been to high-ranking universities, all English literature graduates, ridiculously over-educated to be writing magazines for 12 year olds, but a lot of the best things are written by people who are pitching way over the heads of the people they are writing for . . . Neil Tennant was the assistant editor when I was editor, a fantastically clever and educated person, who worked literary and cultural references into his writing, political references, treating the audience as adults almost, even though it was written in a very straightforward way, simply even . . . this was probably as close as a lot of readers came to literature, they probably didn't read much else apart from *SH*, and I thought that was quite good. We were up against *NME*, which was written by people a lot younger than us a lot of the time and I think while we were making quite complex things simple and legible, they were often making quite simple things extremely complicated, and over-academic . . . there was a great tendency at the *NME* to over-dignify some substandard music, granting tremendous levels of cultural reference and authority to stuff which didn't really merit it.

If Ellen seems to underestimate his audience's reading habits, he also makes an important point about how *Smash Hits* took a chance on contextualising complex ideas against the apparent simplicities of the pop formula while the traditional job of the music press was to talk things up – to make the simple thing seem complex. This connection of supposed 'high' and 'low' cultures was in itself innovative. It is partly a generational issue – these writers had grown up in the 1950s and 1960s, being both sure of the cultural significance of pop music while also being amused and entertained by it. This new style of analysis, double-edged with affectionate praise and reductive satire, was a consequence of these two approaches. So who were these writers and where did they take these innovations?

ME: A lot of the people who worked on *The Face*, a very influential magazine, came from the *Smash Hits* stable – *The Face* was
launched out of our office – Nick Logan didn't have the money
to hire an office so because he'd started *SH* and we were by then
very successful we just let him have 'the room at the end' and
that's where *The Face* was launched and it was designed by the
designer of *SH*, and it was written by people like myself, David
Hepworth, Dave Rimmer, Neil Tennant, so a lot of that writing
then graduated into a slightly older readership, so the influences
spread in that kind of way too.

PM: So writing about the same music but with different
emphases?

ME: Yes that's quite right – Ian Birch, who was the other editor,
went on to become the most successful editor, you might say,
in the world as he was editor of the American *TV Guide*, the
biggest circulation publication on the planet, and launched loads
of magazines at EMAP while I was working with him there so I
suppose we were quite an interesting bunch of people who went
on to do a phenomenal range of things!

Thus the success of *Smash Hits*, and indeed the production of it,
mirrors that of the music it chose to spotlight – a reader might assume
that the writer shared their enthusiasm for the music yet to some extent
this was a confidence trick. To the writers, this was just another job to
try and make a success of. Almost by accident, they succeeded spectacularly. One way in which music magazine publishing mirrors the industry it documents is the emergence of the copycat title – just as within
twelve months of Amy Winehouse's breakthrough success with *Back
to Black* there were a dozen similar female vocal acts being marketed
by competing companies, so an innovative successful magazine will
swiftly spawn imitators even more quickly. Thus titles such as *Number
One* and *Flexipop* soon arrived. The latter anticipated the advent of the
free covermount CD, and the commercial advantages that that offers,
by including a free 'flexidisc' featuring an exclusive track by a popular
act every week – Soft Cell, XTC and the Jam all had tracks issued with
Flexipop. Clearly there was a large market for this new kind of writing
about pop, but by 1985 Mark Ellen had had another idea.

PM: So how did *Q* come to develop out of the success of *Smash
Hits*?

ME: In some ways they were related because they were produced
and edited with the same sensibilities and a lot of the same writers

but the basic difference was that the unit of currency of *SH* was the single, built around the idea that the reader – and acts – concentrated all their efforts and interests around the hit single. In 1985 the feeling was there was going to be a boom in the albums market, and there wasn't actually a monthly music magazine at the time, amazing as it sounds. A whole generation of people had grown up with the weekly music habit so we knew the appetite was there, but what if there was a monthly magazine, which would give you the various advantages of higher quality paper, more durable photographic images, a little more conjecture, a lot more reviews? *Q* was originally based round a review section of over 140 reviews a month, that was going to be the chassis and everything else was to be the icing on the cake, all the stories and the interviews and the humour was just a bonus – we thought we were going to sell to an audience who would buy it because they felt they needed the review section. So the unit around which the whole thing was based was the CD, which was the other really important thing that happened, the invention of the compact disc.

The shift in the main unit of currency from the single to the compact disc was the surface detail of a massive technological revolution not only in how popular music was packaged and consumed but also in how it was produced – the move from analogue to digital. A short piece in *Sounds* in 1974 reported that scientists at Sony in Japan were working on a system that would enable an album's worth of music to be placed on a disc the size of a single ('Don't tell Yes' was the sign-off line) and while discs by Abba and the Bee Gees were pressed up for demonstration purposes in the late 1970s and early 1980s, it wasn't until 1983 that the system was launched onto the marketplace, in an excellent example of 'vertical integration', with Billy Joel's album for Sony *52nd Street* alongside Sony's CDP-101 player. This changed the way people listened to music, how they stored it and what they expected from the source material. As a teenager I never listened to my second-hand copies of albums such as the Beatles' *Revolver*, Bob Dylan's *Blonde on Blonde* and the Young Rascals' *Groovin'* and thought 'this would be so much better if that hi-hat cymbal was a little brighter'. I just loved the sound, pumping out of my cheap record player's speakers. With the advent of digital audio, the consumer was suddenly obliged to take into consideration the perceived quality of that sound – in an old-fashioned term, the elevation of high-fidelity had been reset on the mountain top. Thus such sonic verities became a marketing angle – this is a superior product, with a superior price tag. CDs initially retailed in the

UK at anything up to £15, at a time when vinyl equivalents cost around £5. So the promise of much-improved sound quality became central to persuading people to buy their favourite albums all over again. No forty year old was going to be excessively interested in Adam and the Ants, so if a music magazine wanted to draw in those whom Mark Ellen described as having grown up with their 'weekly music habit' then here was something of an open goal – a valid way of writing about old music, rendered fresh by a new technology and of interest to an older readership with a disposable income.

> *ME:* We figured out – not that it was hard to figure it out – that what would happen is that people were going to go back and re-buy records they already owned on vinyl in this incredible new format and in so doing would reactivate their interest in the life stories and career arcs of these particular people. So I used to run a lot of editorial every month which would be 'the Big Interview' with Eric Clapton, Elton John, Van Morrison, Paul McCartney . . . all these people who were absolutely dead in the water, nobody wrote about them, because they didn't fit into the scheme of things at the *NME* or the *MM*, for whom these characters were well past their heydays and headed for ignominious retirement. So these acts were fantastically cooperative . . . you can't get interviews with many of them now, but then . . . Elton John was falling over himself to give us an exclusive, for someone to take him seriously. So we really made hay, and it succeeded in a very short time, and it [*Q*] took off very quickly.

Mark Ellen's claims about the status of the 1960s peer group of musicians might seem somewhat far-fetched in 2012 but are true at least as far as the music press goes; none of this generation were getting any coverage in the weeklies – why should they? – and pre-Internet, pre-digital communications, and long before the mainstream daily newspapers took an interest in pop beyond gossipy material, they were still wholly dependent upon the printed music press for such publicity. I wondered if this all somehow tied in with the growing narratives surrounding older musicians as their careers and back catalogues grew: how popular music – the postwar quicksilver celebration of the 'now' – had acquired a history.

> *PM:* So where the weeklies had a necessary emphasis on what's happening right now, or what might be interesting in the immediate future if you want be a little ahead of the game, a

magazine like *Q*, which takes the current scene on via reviews and so on, also illuminates the stories of where all this stuff came from makes those connections and gives the subject a history?

ME: That last point, about history, is an excellent one and the most important one to make about *Q* or any of the other titles I've worked on since, really. I was at the *NME* when punk happened, in 76/77. Then, a completely artificial line was drawn in the sand and it was said that 'everything starts now'. So I'd go out and interview the Clash and I was well aware – we were the same age – that they all had musical histories, grown up listening to 60s music, glam rock, Krautrock, whatever, they didn't just come out of the box fully formed . . . you were actively discouraged from not making any genealogical connections, no family tree style references to the old age of rock music as it was seen then, with a few exceptions – you were allowed to write about Iggy Pop as he was deemed to be the Godfather of Punk. Lou Reed, David Bowie . . . but no one else seemed to have a future.

What *Q* did was to open up this idea that rock history was this glorious story with all these chapters started in 1955, and that everything was interconnected, so that what happened in 1962 influenced what happened in 1968 which then impacted upon events in 1972 . . . no one had looked at this that way before. We also looked at the career arcs of these people which I found fascinating. Bob Dylan had to make his mediocre, directionless albums in the 80s in order to reach *Oh Mercy*. It was a complete fiction to take his backstory and narrow it down to a very limited number of records that the *NME* decided to adopt and pronounce worthy, where they fit into their own philosophy and where they don't they just ignore them all!

One of the features of the digital music market was the co-presence of a whole range of an artist's material – David Bowie was the first artist to have his whole back catalogue reissued in this new format, as early as 1985, the 1968 and the 1984 albums sitting beside each other on the rack – the complete works on the shelf. It was an invitation to explore that whole 'arc' as described by Mark Ellen. The CD also made a great volume of hard-to-find material current and freely available in a way that vinyl did not.

PM: The CD's impact was also about stuff simply being available wasn't it . . . suddenly you could find all this stuff, all in the same place, no more scouring second-hand vinyl shops . . .

ME: That's so true, and you can imagine how I felt . . . it was the best job in the world! Who am I going to write about? Is it Richard Thompson? Or XTC? Or even a then-relatively new band like the Jesus and Mary Chain? They've all got a history, and all benefited hugely one way or another from the compact disc. Also, to be a little more tetchy if I may, people were initially mesmerised by the sonic quality of the CD, the whole thing was that it took out the crackle, the surface noise, and we wrote pieces about what you could hear on them, I remember David Hepworth wrote a most marvellous piece on how you could hear the buzz on the string of Keith Richards' guitar, you felt like you were in the room with them, and that old fashioned idea of putting the headphones on and listening to music very closely and acutely reawakened people's interest in those musicians and how that music was made.

This level of attentiveness to the actual technical details of the sound was important – *Q* had for several years a 'hi-fi' review section – and the magazine understood that this new market rested in some way on the technical details as much as the musical content. This, as Ellen notes, made *Q* the transitional publication for the UK music market.

ME: We were just making hay, while others were still struggling with this other agenda, as to how this fits in with our world view, on the campus, which is where all that was aiming, still. I felt we had an open goal really, I didn't feel like we had any competitors. Although we fairly soon did actually, every time we launched a magazine IPC would launch a rival a few months later, we launched *SH* they launched *Number One*, we launched *Q* and they launched something called *Vox*, then *Uncut* which was their answer to *Mojo* . . . I'm waiting for their response to *Word* actually [laughs], it's been going for years now I don't know what's the matter with them! I think a lot of the success of *Q* came from us crediting the readership with the intelligence and appetite for something different.

Ellen's claims to 'credit the readership with intelligence and the appetite for something different' echo his earlier feeling about the inclusiveness of the signature style of *Smash Hits*. This is a central element in the publications in which he is involved – a kind of connoisseurial encoding which fosters a sense of loyalty to the title, the style, the writers. Hence over time a reader will migrate and follow these aspects from title to title as the editors and writers do likewise. Ellen tried to buck this trend somewhat with his next move, a title called *Select* (1990–2000) which spanned the 1990s, not quite knowing where to lay its money down – rock? Dance? "Indie-Dance"? Modern or heritage acts? It had the disadvantage of launching at a time notable only for the fairly low-ebb era of pop it was obliged to document. Ellen described it as 'like the B-side to *Q*, a totally different thing, an early 90s alternative to *Q* really'. It clung feverishly to Britpop, but the magazine is the one failure in this story, and when the editorship was passed to John Harris *Select* went down fast and it barely survived the decade of its inception.

Meanwhile, Mark Ellen had founded another title which took the universal heritage aspects of *Q* onto a yet more connoisseurial level: *Mojo*. First published in 1993, it was unashamedly historical in content, featuring the Beatles, Bob Dylan, the Who and Bruce Springsteen on its cover many times, displaying sound business sense as ABC figures (which record magazine sales) show clearly that these front covers sell their respective issues. But what was the logic behind launching a title like this in the days of grunge and very early Britpop?

ME: Well with *Mojo*, the difference there was that *Q* was a main-stream publication and when we launched *Mojo* at EMAP there was a lot of pressure on us to have some commercial success, they were very much driven by the idea of something which was going to bring a return – *Q* made a lot of money, still does actually – so when we went to present *Mojo*, I was asked to present it to the board and the idea was that this was going to be a cult magazine. I can remember saying 'this will cost you £4million', which it did, and also that 'we will pay that money back quite quickly, but it will never be a mainstream success like *Q* magazine, and shouldn't be judged against *Q*. It was in a parallel universe to *Q* – what it was intended to do, in terms of the company's profile, was to cover EMAP with glory because this was going to be very credible, and very cool, and very authoritative and a very critically respected publication which would make EMAP as publisher look pretty good, rather like the image of Condé Nast supplied by the *New Yorker*.

It cost £4m to launch, which is very little money actually, and I can remember them saying to me when I presented the magazine to them, the board of EMAP said 'who are these readers?' and I said 'I know all of them personally, their names and addresses!' and they thought this was very encouraging. In fact they got their money back very quickly indeed – it broke even in thirteen months which was phenomenal you know? And the great irony of all this is that for a little cult magazine which is meant to be aimed at people with a very specialist interest in rock music . . . so by the time the CD catalogues had really developed it wasn't just a case of going back and buying records you really liked it was going back vertically, exploring right back to the beginning, with some artists you'd maybe never heard of before . . . so people were going back and looking at things that had a certain aesthetic quality to them, very singer-songwriter, mainly cult acts I suppose, some are mainstream now, but not then . . . so it was for people who'd followed the career paths of these artists but also newcomers . . . really in depth.

We ran a piece on Frank Zappa . . . Zappa died actually just as we'd finished the third issue, and I'd decided to put him on the cover of the fourth issue and it was an unbelievable runaway commercial success, because nobody else was doing that, recognising Frank Zappa as being significant in 1994 . . . so it was quite different. And it was designed differently, by a brilliant graphic designer called Andy Cowells – when we were working on the early layouts he asked me 'what sort of a magazine do you think this is?', and I replied 'it's kind of handcut'. I was working on this piece about The Band so showed him this picture of them, around the time of their second album, backwoodsmen kind of thing, in the mountains.

PM: Sepia toned . . .

ME: Sepia toned, exactly, and he said, oh, right and disappeared, and came back about half an hour later and started busying himself in the corner, he'd been out and bought a load of lino, and he was physically handcutting from the lino patterns and headlines to print onto the page! It was a handcrafted thing, a real labour of love. We used to call it the most expensive fanzine on the block.

Of course *Mojo* was not a fanzine – had it been so, it would not have had the advantages of the colour pictures, the luxurious paper – the first issues of the magazine are a tactile treat, silken paper, deep and saturated colour photographs, the aesthetics of luxury realised in a magazine. *Mojo* addressed the apparently boundless availability of music as the CD catalogues Ellen cites were growing way beyond the guaranteed sellers and the mainstream market for rebuying worn vinyl. It also facilitated the embedding of a rock canon beyond the usual special cases of Beatle, Dylan and Rolling Stone recordings.

PM: It seems to me these magazines do provide a way in for acts on the margins to get a way in, a foot in the door as it were, via these magazines which have this connoisseurial gloss to them, and that transfers itself to the act so that someone like Tom Waits who would never be mainstream in the broadest sense is still now a commercial success and a publication like *Mojo*, initially at least, helped these people get their reward, the recognition, the status and also the sales.

ME: Well you're absolutely right . . . Jeff Buckley is a good example, perhaps. *Grace* was a masterpiece, out of nowhere! But a rock press had been invented that could take those fringe artists seriously and devote time and space to them . . . one of the differences between these titles we're talking about is that *Q* was there to reflect the commercial hierarchy, so that means if someone sells a lot of records, you have an obligation to cover them, so that, for example, Queen would get as much coverage as, say, Dylan or a more cult artist and ultimately I learned from that experience that that was probably the wrong way to do it, even for *Q*. If an act sells 300,000 albums, then there should be an available pool of people who might want to read about them, but that isn't how it works. Phil Collins sold hundreds of thousands of records in that era but his audience were only slightly interested in him as a person, he didn't have a specialist audience, whereas Tom Waits or the Smiths, who didn't sell many records in the early days, had a level of interest that was absolutely enormous! So I very soon discovered that while certain people may not have an enormous commercial draw, they are the ones with the most devoted followings – those are the ones who are going to be the big commercial engines for magazines.

It was only at the end of my time at *Q* that I worked this out, I felt like I had a moral obligation to write about Fleetwood Mac or Tracy Chapman or whoever was flavour of the month because they were just so popular I felt duty bound to do it! Yet you didn't get much return from that kind of thing . . . I kept going back to the people who sold. That was what happened at the *NME* when I was there . . . The Clash didn't actually sell many records at the beginning, you'd go to see them on the south coast and they weren't even filling their venues, but they were selling 200–250,000 copies of a weekly newspaper, so they were selling five times as many papers as they were records! This tells you that the folklore of the Clash was somehow more marketable than their music!

The rewriting of history is pertinent – the UK's biggest selling acts of 1977 were the Bee Gees, Abba and Leo Sayer but you'd never know that from the cultural histories made of that year. Yet as Ellen notes, acts such as these had in the main audiences who were satisfied with the pleasure the music provided and did not necessarily have a hunger for deeper analysis or personal details of the sort craved by Smiths or Tom Waits aficionados, for example. Ellen's example, the Clash, illustrates the transformative power of writing about music, in that acts who were not particularly revered in their own time come to assume great retrospective significance. This can also be said of Nick Drake, Joy Division and, further back, the Velvet Underground. Mark Ellen had a sensitive observation to make about this phenomenon:

> *ME*:   Yes I always think there's a connection with some of the 70s people, people like Roy Harper [1970s singer-songwriter] and so on, their presence in the press and perceived significance was totally unrelated to their record sales which were always very low, but these guys are now burdened with enormous fame, but very little financial reward for it. Same for members of the Damned.

This icily illustrates the difference between the type of cultural value placed upon an artist and their work by the mediation of the music press and how that critical acclaim translates (or not) into commercial reward. We are reminded of Nick Drake's late song 'Hanging on a Star', a tune which Joe Boyd has several times asserted was a direct response to the shortfall Drake saw between what people told him about his musical talents and the almost complete indifference of the record buying public to his work in his lifetime (see Boyd 2006). There is little virtue in the high praise of a journalist when one is penniless.

By the time he left *Mojo*, Ellen really had nowhere left to go in terms of chasing down the traditional routes of music writing and publishing – his innovations had become standard practice, adopted right across the growing music magazine market – consider how closely magazines covering classical music or jazz or folk resemble the models he laid down at *Q* and *Mojo*. Five years divided the end of his tenure at *Mojo* and the launch of his next project, *The Word*, in September 2003. I asked him about the purpose of his returning to the magazine market and his ambitions for the title.

> *PM*:   *The Word* began trying to offer a wider cultural view rather than just being a music magazine – am I right?

ME: Definitely, and I'll tell you the reason for that – or one of the many reasons for it – this is a magazine aimed at people over 30, 35, right up to their 50s and 60s even, and it's aimed at people with a very clear understanding of what they like and what they don't like . . . you can sell *NME* to a load of people who are suggestible, really, they're impressionable and you can convince them to like something because it's fashionable. The readers of *Word* are older and wiser and they kind of know what they like, grumpy old men and women if you like, and they know what conforms to their tastes and standards and what doesn't, and part of the reason that it's not just about music is that in order to interest and entertain them then music is probably not going to be able to supply everything every month, and also that much of the music we write about is informed by the broader popular cultural landscape . . . the books that people are writing, the films that are being made. . . so that's one of the reasons.

The Word was indeed initially pitched as a kind of latter-day *Rolling Stone*, taking in a wider cultural range – ironically, just as the *NME* had done before punk – such as film, books and observations of popular culture in general: its original strapline was 'At last . . . something to *read*!', emphasising the writing rather than the promotional content. It was good, but often read like a trade publication – the 'insider' model which had yielded such great rewards at *Smash Hits*, *Q* and *Mojo* had here been reduced down to a language which often felt as if it were directed toward a small group of media professionals – not unlike a consumer version of *Music Week*. This limited its appeal as a commercial concern and the magazine struggled for a while until it shifted toward music as its core concern and is now firmly a music title. Surprisingly, it sometimes bears an aggressively conservative tone, appearing suspicious of innovation. Perhaps this is appropriate, however, as *Word* is possibly the logical end-point for this kind of print-based music journalism – the original generation of writers and consumers are now well into middle age and freer mediations of responses to popular music are firmly established – the blog, free of editorial control, being merely the most obvious example. I asked Mark Ellen how he envisaged the future for his own magazine and for the wider industry:

PM: What's your view of *Word*'s virtual presence? The website is very busy with podcasts, message boards and so on – which way do you see the magazine going? Will there be a stereo separation of hard copy and online versions?

ME: One of the reasons so much effort was put into the website is that a monthly frequency just seemed slow, it always did in a way but now seems even slower in a world where there isn't any news. This is the problem for the monthly market in the last ten years or so . . . the monthly market was powered by the fact that you were publishing news – facts that people didn't know. Now of course, every single fact is leeched out of the source very early on and there's nothing that people don't already know . . . if the Smiths are reforming they already know that, they're not going to find that out from the cover of a magazine! So a month seems like a very long time, when during that month the readership of a magazine like ours have just soaked up vast amounts of knowledge and opinion, so the effort was put into the website to try and create this community, where the magazine fed into the website and the website fed back into the magazine and so it goes on, keeping that whole idea of a community and debate alive, kindred spirits connected in this virtual world. It keeps them in touch with the world of the magazine and keeps their interest in the magazine up, and we then hope they will carry on buying the paper version of it. I say virtual world, we've had two instances of contributors to the website organising parties in pubs where they all meet up and occasionally invite us along – it used to be the other way round, a magazine would have a party and a lucky reader might get to go . . . now the readers arrange parties and we're lucky if we get to go! That's got to be a good sign!

Here we see the natural endpoint of the line of continuity that has run through all the titles we have examined here – the effort to keep readers loyal by creating a community. Now the competition isn't a handful of similar titles but the unceasing flow of information, from the individual artists' websites to MSN News. The core readership now claim not only membership of an elite club – just like the kids poring over their Duran Duran posters and composing letters to *Smash Hits* – but also a kind of proprietorial claim, a form of ownership of the 'idea' of the magazine and a shared belief system as to what is important. I asked whether he would ever consider publishing a magazine exclusively online:

ME: Well I don't know if that's a decision that's particularly up to us really . . . it's up to the way things are going to pan out. I'd like to ask that question to Rupert Murdoch! He's investigating paying millions to put tons of stuff online and charge for it, it's a huge subject, but obviously if people are getting vast amounts of information and entertainment they used to pay for in print free online then by rights it should be possible to try and monetise that; but as far as I personally am concerned, I think this system [as employed by *The Word*] works really well and I appreciate that ALL magazines are under pressure because there's a bit of an advertising drought at the moment but I also firmly believe, in fact I can be tiresomely evangelical about this, that print media offers you various characteristics that are absolutely inimitable, unique and irreplaceable. It's pretty obvious what they are; you can edit your reading of a magazine anyway you want to, you can publish an editorial with depth and perspective that you just can't take on board if you're reading off a screen or if it's coming to you via other broadcast media, such as TV or radio. These magazines are the only medium for substantial, three-dimensional journalism I think. You can read it and re-read it twice if you want to, here's the diagram, look at the picture, construct the whole story in your head . . . there's also something very attractive I think about the paper product!

Mark Ellen's final comment is important – the old-fashioned media has survived not only because of its convenience or otherwise, but because of its apparently infinite adaptability, and the tactile pleasures of holding and exploring a three-dimensional artefact as opposed to an image on a screen. Just as a box of love letters beats a bundle of printed e-mails or the memory of a text message, they are cherishable and tangible evidence that the past once was. As Ellen said to me, 'you can collect them, re-read them, they have a real value and a real place in our lives, and I fondly hope that isn't going to disappear.' The next few years will prove this to have been true or the final phase of this kind of writing about popular culture. What's certain is that the way popular music is written about in the UK publishing market would have been very different without the influence and input of Mark Ellen, and readers, writers and the music industry itself all have reason to thank him for that.

The daily newspaper journalist – Laura Barton, *The Guardian*

Laura Barton is a journalist who joined *The Guardian* in 2002. She has written about a whole range of topics, both musical and non-musical

in content, but is perhaps best known for the fortnightly column
'Hail, Hail, Rock'n'Roll'. She left the paper as a full-time employee
in early 2010, although she still contributes to it on a regular basis
including 'HHRNR'. She has also made programmes for BBC Radio
4 and is a Contributing Editor to *Q* magazine. In July 2010 she published her first novel, *Twenty One Locks*. I asked her about her career
and the relationship between popular music and the daily, mainstream
news press.

> *PM*:   How and where did you begin writing about music?
>
> *LB*:   I did little bits and bobs of writing about music when I was
> at school and sixth form – I remember answering the essay topic
> of 'How I Spent My Summer Holidays' with a detailed account
> of how I had spent the six-week stretch of holiday falling in love
> with the Pixies' song 'Hey'. Later I edited the sixth-form maga-
> zine and occasionally wrote pieces on music, and I wrote for a
> couple of trifling things for fanzines, and later for my university
> student paper [Barton attended Worcester College, Oxford]. But
> largely I viewed music as too precious to write about, or perhaps
> I felt I wasn't quite ready to write about something so dear to me,
> and so it wasn't until I joined *The Guardian* that I began writing
> about it properly.
>
> *PM*:   Was music part of your remit when you arrived at *The
> Guardian*?
>
> *LB*:   No, not at all. I joined *The Guardian* straight after university
> – in fact I was offered my job before I sat my finals, and the
> editor who hired me was the Features editor. He had very spe-
> cific ideas about what I should and shouldn't write about, and
> for some reason he saw writing about music as a kind of waste
> of my writing. I did odds and sods of course, because they knew
> that I knew a lot about music. And then I think his opinion
> began to change when I did an interview with Johnny Borrell of
> Razorlight.

Barton's observation that someone the paper thought highly of – being
hired as a journalist before even graduating – would be regarded as
wasting their talent on writing about music is startling, given how
much space popular music occupies in the contemporary British
mainstream press. It reveals something of how such a publication is
constructed – that they might prioritise material that they feel they
ought to include to 'appease' their readership rather than believing it
worthy of skilful scrutiny. The mixed reputation of music journalism

may also have something to do with this – we recall that Frank Zappa referred to music journalism as being 'written by people who can't write for people who can't read'. So when a talented writer like Laura Barton is sufficiently interested in such a subject then something interesting may well begin to happen.

> *PM*: How did you come to be asked to write the fortnightly column 'Hail, Hail, Rock'n'Roll'?
>
> *LB*: Around 2003/4 I became good friends with Michael Hann, an editor on another section of the paper, and a large part of our friendship was based on a shared love for rock'n'roll. He worked in another building, and we would often e-mail one another at great length about favourite lyrics, or our passion for Jonathan Richman, and the like. Occasionally we made one another mix CDs. And a while after we started going to gigs, or first discovering that we'd been at the same gigs. And then we began a club night together.
>
> A couple of years later, Michael was appointed editor of the *Guardian*'s Film & Music section, and he set about implementing a redesign, which would include a new music columnist. I remember we discussed this column at length, with me making suggestions for people who might be good, and he tried out an awful lot of people. It never occurred to me that I might even be a contender, since I never saw myself as a columnist, plus I knew there were many other music writers who had written for the section for a lot longer. However, shortly before the redesign Michael begged me to write the column, since unbeknownst to me what he had been hoping to launch was a column that was very much like our e-mails about music – very intimate, and less cynical than most music columns, something that could convey the joy we feel about rock'n'roll.

Barton's good fortune was to connect with a like-minded fellow journalist and between them they were able to make something new happen – as she says, 'Hail, Hail, Rock'n'Roll' is distinguished by its approach to the subject, which owes little to the tone or vocabularies of established music journalism. There is a sense of freedom of form and a lightness even when the topic feels 'heavy'. The example reproduced in the appendix of this book is a good example of this process. I wondered whether her obligation as a mainstream journalist to write about a whole range of topics helped her to write in this new way about music.

PM: Do you consider yourself a journalist who writes occasionally about music, or a music writer who also works on a wider range of subjects?

LB: Increasingly the latter. I generally tell people that about 50 per cent of what I do is music writing, but in truth it's where my heart lies. I'm happy to write about other subjects, but it never makes me as happy as writing about music. I think the only thing that comes close is when I'm writing about nature. I feel a similar sense of awe for both subjects.

PM: Do you have to negotiate for your music-based content in *The Guardian* or can you submit ideas as you wish?

LB: For my column I can write whatever I please really. For bigger articles it really works both ways – sometimes I get asked to do things, and other times I pitch them. It's sometimes tricky to keep G2 sweet at the same time as writing music articles. They get a bit grumpy about it. But they also ask me to write any music pieces that come up – though they tend to be foisted upon me rather than the music I love.

Clearly there is a trade-off here, where the writer has a certain 'space' in which she can 'write whatever I please, really' but also finds that material is 'foisted upon' her. Furthermore her employer wished that she would place more emphasis on her non-musical output. Her mentioning of nature as something which inspires a 'similar awe' to music points to both her view of music as something fit for celebration ('Hail, Hail . . .') rather than cynicism but also connects it to the wider world of experience and not confined to a prescribed corner where it is kept in its place. Her 2009 *Guardian* series 'Barton's Britain', which also had an online life as a series of short films which developed and complemented the written pieces, is a good example of how her writing reaches up under the influence of nature as powerfully as it does when focusing upon music. I wondered if in order to write well about a piece of music she had to like it a good deal.

PM: Is there a style or manner of music which appeals to you as a subject in particular?

LB: To be honest I love a really broad selection of music – 50s rock'n'roll to punk to pop. I mean I'll happily dance to Girls Aloud and Chuck Berry played back to back. But I readily admit that I have some kind of natural affinity for slightly melancholic and what you might call lyrically-governed music, often with a more acoustic leaning – Van Morrison, Bob Dylan, Bill

Callahan, Bon Iver, Bonnie 'Prince' Billy, Cat Power, Joanna Newsome. But I love garage rock and a nice bit of AC/DC too.

Some of these names appear in her columns and some don't but what is clear is that what interests her isn't necessarily governed by genre or indeed age. Her working definition of 'slightly melancholic . . . lyrically-governed music . . . with an acoustic leaning' covers a lot of ground, from the blues onward. This can be of benefit to artist as well as listener and reader, of course – for example, as she notes later, her eloquent advocacy of the work of Justin Vernon who records as 'Bon Iver' had a great impact upon his success in the UK. So I wondered how this new way of writing about pop related to what she had read in the press and magazines as a consumer rather than a producer.

> *PM*: Did you read music magazines or weeklies while you were growing up?
>
> *LB*: Oh yes! First *Look-in*, and then *Smash Hits*, in its heyday, which I loved. Then *Q*, because it was written by all the *Smash Hits* bods. And *Select*, and then *Mojo* and many, many others. I pretty much spent all my pocket money/Saturday job earnings on music magazines and records. Interestingly, perhaps, I never liked the *NME*. Maybe it was just the time – it was particularly gnarly then, but it was the cynicism and the vitriol I couldn't stand, or indeed relate to how much I loved music. I read it to know the bands, but that was really all.

In this reply her enthusiasm and wide reading in the form seems to have both grounded her writing in the styles available to the pop writer but also showed her clearly what she didn't want to do – that is, the model of rock and pop journalism as embodied by the *NME* of the early to mid-1990s. What grew out of this mediocre era was an increased presence of popular music in the daily mainstream news press as a subject fit for consideration and focus, and allowed journalists like Laura Barton to mix specifically music-related work with more traditional newspaper topics.

> *PM*: In the 1970s and 80s pop music was largely only covered by specialist publications – how and why do you think dailies now offer such comprehensive coverage, and what impact has this had on the specialist market?
>
> *LB*: I'm not sure when exactly . . . probably in the mid-90s, and I would imagine it had to do with a generational shift, with the fact

that now this generation of men and women who were perhaps the first to grow up thoroughly steeped in popular music had become the writers and editors of mainstream publications. That may not be true. But I think it definitely has something to do with popular music becoming acceptable and widespread while these people were growing up, and so it would be hard to keep it as an underground 'youth' phenomenon. Maybe also punk in that way had a lot to do with it – that generation which came of age and documented the punk movement in the late 70s and early 80s would probably be reaching positions of authority by the 90s.

Barton is correct in identifying this generational shift and evidence is everywhere; for example, Courtney Love was asked to chair an editorial meeting at *The Guardian* in 2009 and musicians are frequently consulted on matters of the day in the press or on television shows such as the BBC's *Question Time*. Following on from this, we might consider how a writer might switch between registers of expertise and those suited to a more general readership; there is a range of assumptions of reader knowledge – musical styles, personal narratives – which a writer for a specialist magazine can draw upon which are not necessarily present in the audience for a daily paper.

> *PM*: Do you change register between publications, so that you write one way for, say *Q* or *The Word*, another for *The Guardian*? What is the difference between writing for a specialist publication and a daily newspaper?
>
> *LB*: In a lot of ways, yes I do change my voice, if we can call it that. It's nice writing for specialist press because you don't have to explain everything. I remember writing an interview with the Kings of Leon for the *Guardian* Weekend magazine, and the editor called up and asked me who the Allman Brothers were. That kind of thing is frustrating. There are frustrations writing for magazines too – they tend to be staffed by men, and particularly men of a certain generation. It's quite boys clubby, and the kind of writing favoured is probably that heyday *Q*-era style, which I love, but it's not what I do really. However, I know that's more what they want me to deliver. The writing that I enjoy most and that feels the most 'me' is the HHRNR column, and in part that's because I have an editor I trust.

Here, via the unlikely case of 1970s US rockers the Allman Brothers, we see the distance between the domains of specialist music writing and the perceived obligation of the dailies to offer coverage of the same music. Yet as she notes, the music magazine world has its own rules and essentially conservative infrastructures too. It is the task of the journalist, much of the time, to deal with and write about topics which aren't necessarily 'me', as Laura Barton puts it. How does a writer deal with this?

> *PM*:   Some writers have mentioned to me that occasionally they struggle while interviewing/writing about music they do not care for – how do you deal with this apparent difficulty?
>
> *LB*:   Oh lord, it's difficult. I don't have to do it too often, thankfully, but sometimes I just run out of things to say or ask or whatever. It's a lot easier in a funny way if they're some sort of pop phenomenon, because then it becomes a bit of a dance, or there's more to play with, or it can be a comedy. I find it hardest if they're some hip new band, some next big thing, and you have to speak to the whole band en masse, and they're deadly earnest, but you don't really passionately love their music and it's hard to muster enthusiasm, somehow, you know?

Traditionally the British music press did not need to make these leaps of the imagination – indeed part of the point of papers like the *NME* in the 1970s and 1980s was to deflate and denounce as much as it was to praise or promote. So the kind of sustained campaigns mounted by the *NME* against the likes of Bryan Ferry in the 1970s and Morrissey in the early 1990s simply could not happen in the pop coverage provided by the daily press. There is a changed dynamic between the music industry and the people who write about it. Furthermore, this kind of negative campaigning cannot be conducted in the monthlies, who unfailingly give positive write-ups to their interviewees. A contemporary writer on pop has to be ready to formulate and express considered opinions on music they do not necessarily like. This reins in of some of the most passionate writing that has distinguished pop journalism, but also seems like a good thing too – the music, not the journalist, has to be the focus. I wondered how this shift in the power balance toward the consumer and the producer, with the journalist now functioning as a kind of mediator rather than arbiter of taste, has altered the cultural status of the music writer:

> *PM*:   Can music journalists working today be as powerful as taste makers and 'cultural gatekeepers' as writers in the 1970s/1980s undoubtedly were?

LB: Well, I suppose readers, listeners and watchers have more options now, more things to read, the whole Internet at their fingertips, giant record stores, iTunes, Amazon, a million publications, an increased quantity of reader-generated content . . . and in some ways that's great and massively exciting. In others it means it's a lot of voices to listen to. I think music writers still can be very important though – you know, *Pitchfork* maybe proofs that pudding. And I think great authoritative, intelligent criticism still stands and has an important role. I don't know how powerful my role makes me, but I do know I get a phenomenal response when I write something, and I know it does generate sales . . . Bon Iver is, I guess, a case in point in my own career.

The rise of a great clamour of voices is in direct opposition to the music weekly model where the journalist's voice was unchallenged and the readers' letters page was the only place in which the consumer could have a say. Presently, as Laura Barton notes, there is an almost unlimited array of places to read about popular music and one could read a score of wildly differing opinions on any recording with a single Internet search. This idea of 'reader-generated content' has destabilised the authoritative assumptions surrounding the music journalist and, as Mark Ellen noted, this can extend to the point where a magazine like *The Word* seems to be more about being a meeting place, virtually or in the real world, for consumers than it does about actual scrutiny of content. Yet Barton is quite correct in asserting that 'authoritative, intelligent criticism' still has 'an important role', citing the online magazine *Pitchfork*. Art is not entirely understood through the assessment of market value or whether we feel we have had our money's worth.

This issue came up again when I asked about the limits of writing about as opposed to listening and experiencing the music.

PM: Have you ever been defeated by a piece of music while trying to write about it?

LB: Hmmm. No. But I tend to only really tackle a subject if I know what I feel about it, roughly. There's nearly almost always a 'revelation moment' while I'm writing – somehow my brain works better when I'm in the thick of writing, I think, but generally I sit down to write about a piece of music because I want to tell you something about it.

So there is a kind of missionary zeal behind Barton's work which lies at the root of all great critical writing. This 'revelation moment', where one discovers and extrapolates an idea simply by concentrating on it and writing it down connects with novelist E. M. Forster's renowned maxim from *The Art of the Novel* 'How can I know what I think until I see what I say?' (Forster 2009: 24), that is in order to understand what you think about something, you need to write it down – it is not just a case of knowing everything already and just 'downloading' it onto the page. The writing is a creative act, a form of discovery; the mediation is both observation and creativity. Having made this observation, what might be the music journalist's view of other music writing?

PM: What is your favourite piece of writing about music?

LB: It might be something by SFJ [Sasha Frere-Jones of *The New Yorker*]. I loved a piece he wrote about R Kelly in the *New Yorker* a while back. I love how damned thorough he is. I was actually reading another piece of his lately, about Bruno Mars, and trying to pinpoint what I love about his writing. SFJ is a musician himself and I think you can tell that in the rhythm of his writing – rhythm is such an important thing for me in writing, and I love the rhythm he has. But also I think it's a certain precision he has that I admire. He has this obvious vast wealth of knowledge which makes his writing have weight, and seem so unhurried, and his sentences so finely-turned. Plenty of music writers can do that, I know, but SFJ marries it to something else – he'll suddenly deliver a single line that has a warmth or a humour or a particularly arresting image, or something that just seems very human rather than encyclopaedic. The R Kelly piece was a prime example, because it never took the easy route or chose the cheap gags, but rather discussed Kelly's musical contribution while never losing sight of its fundamental amusingness. He writes quite differently to me – I'm more about the sensual effect of the music, a sort of immersion technique or something, I'm more messy and emotional, so I really savour that precision he has.

It might be the bio Peter Robinson wrote about Girls Aloud, in which he linked conveyor-belt pop to Britain's manufacturing history. That was just spectacularly British writing, to me, very different to that SFJ style of broad strokes and precision. It was such a mingling of pride and humility, which I think of as a very British state, and it was funny and moving in a really understated way. I think it might have been because Peter Robinson gets how important pop music is to people – not just to critics and music aficionados, but to the people going out on a Saturday night in Doncaster, the people who make requests on the local radio station, just how pop – in its purest, unapologetically manufactured state – is what soundtracks people's lives. His piece about Girls Aloud was really such a celebration of that, the antithesis of the intellectualised *New Yorker* writing, perhaps, but just as effective, just as heart-winning.

So the combination of writers here is an intriguing one – Sasha Frere-Jones is a critic, free to say what he wishes in theory, and works in the rarefied environment of the *New Yorker* magazine while Barton's other nominated writer, Peter Robinson, performs a PR function. Here we have two distinct worlds of music writing – the cultural gatekeeper and the salesperson. Distinct, yet inextricably linked – the latter may sway the former, and the former may control the levels of success of the latter. They are two aspects of the same process of selling. Barton acknowledges this in her closing observation that both can be 'just as effective' in the process of winning hearts. I wondered if, like musicians, music writers find themselves submitting to their influences and allowing their style to reflect this.

PM: Are you aware of any strong influences upon your writing? They could be other writers or not.

LB: I'm not massively influenced by other music writers. I'm in total awe of other music writers of course, but I don't feel especially influenced by them or in competition with them either. I'd say I'm influenced by certain novelists or poets, and indeed certain lyricists, and funnily I find I can write best to certain songs, which in some way must be an influence. If I'm writing, I'll often listen to one song on repeat, regardless of whether that is the song I am writing about. Recent-ish examples might be James Blake's version of 'A Case of You' or 'Beauty' by the Shivers. I can listen to Bon Iver's *For Emma, Forever Ago*, and quite a few Van Morrison songs, as well as Bob Dylan singing 'You're a Big Girl Now' (the *Biograph* version). I also have this playlist called 'Stolen Car' on my iTunes, which consists only of three songs – Bruce Springsteen's 'Stolen Car', Cat Power's 'I Found a Reason' and Smog's 'Left Only With Love'. If I can't find a song that soothes and settles me enough to write I put that playlist on, on repeat. They're three perfect writing songs, for me. I think actually, looking at the songs I have named the perfect writing songs are all quite melancholy and quite soul-baring, and they all have a point in them, to me, where they kind of reach an emotional peak, and when I get to that point in listening I feel myself unlocking a little, or giving way, or opening up, and that's the state I like to be in when I'm writing. This probably sounds ridiculous, I realise, but it's as if they are songs capable of penetrating the layers, or getting to the raw bit of you, and I think that's where the interesting thoughts, the interesting writing comes from.

The notion that it might cost the writer something – emotionally as well as in time and energy – to produce their copy is, surprisingly, an unusual one in music journalism, which has frequently struggled with a culture of jaded cynicism. There is still that connoisseurial dimension here, specifying a particular version of a Bob Dylan tune, and the repeated use of a certain selection of tunes seems to act as a kind of charm or spell which, as she says, opens up and unlocks the possibilities of responding properly to the music that is under discussion. It's worth noting, too, that the music she listens to at such points is not the music she is writing about.

As the mediation of the written text spread, there was a spillage of the better writers into other media, as the same generational shifts described by Barton have led radio and TV schedules to begin to reflect the history and narratives of popular music cultures – not only in the expected places, such as music stations like the BBC's dedicated channels, but also in the cinema, as subject for documentary and socio-cultural analysis, and talk radio. Barton has written and presented a couple of short shows for BBC Radio 4 discussing lyrics and matters arising with the likes of Jarvis Cocker, and I asked how this had impacted upon the mediation of music via her writing style:

> *PM*: You have also begun contributing music journalism-based programming to BBC radio – how has this new form of delivery changed your writing style?
>
> *LB*: In a funny way it has reinforced it. I've always been really conscious of rhythm in my writing – I want it to sound beautiful, even if you're reading in silence. If that makes any sense at all. One of my biggest complaints in fact when someone edits my work badly is that they lose the rhythm. Writing for radio therefore seems a bit of a gift.

The lack of the internal gatekeeper of the editor or sub-editor seems one of the things which enables her broadcast work to, paradoxically, most closely approach her original ambition and meaning for her writing. The rhythmic sense of a work may well be opaque to someone simply looking for ways to reduce a word count and hence carefully constructed phrases may often be simply pulled apart. In this sense the writing and its possible structures, which are both robust and incredibly fragile, are vulnerable to the same editorial blunders which might be brought to bear upon the music itself. The spoken word – just like the experience of the note sung live to a room – flies free of this kind of mediation and indeed seems 'a bit of a gift'.

Looking ahead, I invited Barton to muse aloud upon both the future and purposes of writing about music:

> *PM*:   Do you have any sense of what lies in the future for the printed music press, and for music journalists?
>
> *LB*:   Honestly? Not massively. I know we have changes afoot, and I know that readers' appetite for music coverage is unlikely to diminish, but where those readers are going to be is shifting online, and so perhaps there will be more blogging, audio, video, or perhaps there will just be more content. I really don't know. I don't even know how relevant the album review will be in an era in which the album might become obsolete . . .

Her candid vexation as to the future of music writing is revealing – like Ellen there is a vague sense that the future will be more online, but how great the percentages will be no one can yet clearly see. Will the cultural authority of the music writer wither and die as we are deluged by the opinions of, well, anybody and everybody? Or will certain titles or styles of writing endure and remain seen as arbiters of taste in the traditional gatekeeper role? Or, as Barton suggests, will the basic building block of rock writing – the album as coherent unified work – simply fade away? How then will the business of writing about music be conducted? To close I asked her two more philosophical questions about the purpose and nature of this endeavour:

> *PM*:   The Czech composer Bohislav Martinu said that writing about music is necessarily adjectival – describing one's response to music rather than the music itself. What do you think about this?
>
> *LB*:   Well, it might be true. But what I've found in the way I write about music, which is very adjectival, is that other people often have a similar response. Also that I think there is some merit, or joy, in writing a beautiful thing about a beautiful thing. If that makes sense. And I suppose also one plays music to create

an adjectival response in oneself and others, or to answer an adjectival need in oneself.

PM: So, what is the purpose of writing about music?

LB: On a wider scale, I don't know, or rather there are a variety of reasons, some to do with refining consumer choice (terrible phrase), some to define a cultural movement, or place a frame around it – which can be both pointless and problematic. I can only really reliably answer in terms of why I write about music, which came out of two friends sharing experience and sharing enthusiasm and beauty, in a daffy kind of way – it came out of something life-affirming, and so when I write about music I'm just trying to extend that same life-affirming enthusiasm to a wider audience. Yes, I realise how soppy that sounds. I guess what I'm saying is that some music writing seems to me like a very Victorian form of botany and I'd rather be a David Attenborough. I'm not sure that answers your question, except to say that the reason I write about music is essentially to say 'wow'.

Writing or reading about music is certainly no substitute for listening to it. However, this 'life-affirming' element Barton describes here (just to say 'wow') is something which can be added to the experience of listening and thus is in itself a kind of mediation, not just of product or of what fashion decrees is good today but perhaps not tomorrow; instead it creates, as she says, something beautiful out of something beautiful and this is what writing about music, at its best, can do. Managing to do it in the pages of a mainstream daily newspaper is exceptional indeed and mark Barton's work out as a possible way forward for the art and craft of writing about popular music and how it might survive.

The niche magazine editor – Simon Broughton of *Songlines*

When we are talking or thinking about music writing in the UK the frequent assumption is that the subject will be pop and/or rock music. This is certainly the case in how the province of the specialist magazines and weeklies has been taken on board by the mainstream daily news press – pop is everywhere but jazz, blues, folk and even classical repertoires, events and performers still have to fight for their place on the review pages; for example, *The Guardian* is involved in the promotion of Glastonbury and Latitude festivals, but does not sponsor a dedicated jazz or a folk event. The case of 'World Music' is even more intriguing in that, almost by definition, its parameters are not clearly fixed in the popular imagination. Interest in this field has developed alongside increased opportunities for travel, the global export and import of music and of course the Internet. In the UK, the plainest examples of this are the World of Music and Dance (or WOMAD) festivals, begun in Somerset in 1982 by Peter Gabriel and which have become a worldwide franchise, and *Songlines* magazine, edited by Simon Broughton, who – cementing that link between travel and World Music cultures – wrote and edited the *Rough Guide to World Music* (1993), the first and still influential comprehensive survey of the field. The magazine, launched in 1999, seeks to document and mediate this newly sprawling global marketplace. It is now firmly established as one of the UK's key music monthlies. I asked Simon Broughton for his views on how the music and the way it is mediated has developed over the decade since the magazine's launch.

PM: When did you first become interested in what has come to be known as 'World Music'?

SB: It started pretty early for me, when I was a teenager – I went on holidays in the summer to Ireland where we heard great music in pubs and I bought things like the Nonesuch Explorer records [a series of indigenous folk albums, usually licensed from state record companies in Africa, Latin America and the former Eastern Bloc].

But the crucial moment for me was going to Hungary in 1978 – because it was cheap and I was interested in what was left of the music that inspired Béla Bartók. I was lucky enough to be introduced to Marta Sebestyen and Muzsikas – I've always had a knack of somehow finding the best people – and they took me to Transylvania in neighbouring Romania where we went to fantastic wedding parties. I had stumbled on a musical culture that was happening every weekend, with glorious musicians on violins and other strings playing gorgeous Transylvanian dances. Not self-conscious folk music, but everyday wedding music with a function.

This notion of 'music with a function' is central to both the way non-Anglophone popular musics are understood and marketed away from their source. These are often, but not always, the 'folk' music of a particular place or region, that is music which has a connection to the rhythms of life as lived day by day in those places and responding to the pleasures and hardships of such a life – music, indeed, with a social function beyond the act of consumption. I asked Simon Broughton about the terminology:

PM: What do you think the term 'World Music' actually means?

SB: The term means different things to different people but as far as I'm concerned – for *Songlines* and the *Rough Guide to World Music* – it is music outside the Anglo-American tradition that has some roots in a local or national culture.

PM: So in relation to this opening up of cultures and exploring the 'otherness', as well as the connections, how influential do you think the *Rough Guide* books (travel and dedicated music titles) and CDs were in fostering the popularity and/or availability of 'World Music' in the UK and beyond?

SB: The books and CDs were very influential, although most important was probably the rise in the live music – at festivals, WOMAD primarily but many others, and at concerts. Over the last decade there has been a huge influx of world music into mainstream concert halls in London and other big cities in the UK. The number of CDs has exploded and because of the CDs and gigs there's been an increasing need for books and publications like *The Rough Guide to World Music* and *Songlines*. The music comes first and then the media which promotes further interest in the music.

Broughton sees that all media relating to musical forms and styles are reactive and responsive – this of course is somewhat at odds with the idea prevalent in rock and pop journalism and magazine publishing, where the imprimatur of the cultural gatekeeper can confer or deny status, distribution and success to one title or artist or another. Broughton may well be modestly underplaying his own role in the dissemination of the music that he writes about in *Songlines* and elsewhere, but it is an intriguing shift in emphasis from the power broking familiar from the pop press. So if a magazine follows the music, I wondered quite where that initial impetus came from.

PM: What was the initial motivation behind launching *Songlines*?

SB: Well *Songlines* wasn't my idea! It was Chris Pollard who ran *Gramophone* magazine, who'd noticed the rise in world music recordings and saw a space in the market for a publication about them. I'd written a letter of complaint to *Gramophone* about a music of Asia supplement they'd published saying that it was stuck in old-fashioned ideas – unchanging traditional music and nothing about the vibrant contemporary popular forms of music. I got a call a few months later saying they were thinking about launching a world music magazine and would I come in to talk to them about it.

PM: Was backing easy to find for the launch of the magazine?

SB: The money for the launch of the magazine wasn't a problem – it was a quarterly spin-off from *Gramophone* and financed by them. The problems came when Haymarket, [Michael] Heseltine's publishing company, bought *Gramophone* and got *Songlines* with it. They decided to stop *Songlines* in autumn 2001 – 9/11 was one of the excuses! But it had made enough of an impression in the world music industry for people to believe it should continue. It took about six months to get two backers and a business plan together. We got the *Songlines* name from Haymarket for £1 and Chris Pollard and Mark Ellingham (founder of the *Rough Guides*) put in the finances. But becoming an independent magazine made a huge difference. We could do our own marketing and partnerships. Since taking over the magazine from Haymarket, our circulation has gone from around 1,500 to 6,000 – a huge increase. But niche magazine publishing isn't lucrative – it's a very fine balance keeping it going. But we do now have five full-time staff, myself (half-time) and a lot of freelance writers.

In the letter to *Gramophone* he mentions here Broughton described the *Rough Guide to World Music* as being 'expressly designed to help people find their way through the maze, with lively and intelligent writing and sensible disc recommendations' (*Gramophone*, July 1996, p. 8) and this is clearly part of what the publishers were looking for in their new magazine project. The full telling of the story of the faltering early days of the magazine illustrates very well how fine the line is between getting a title 'right' in the marketplace and the project coming to nought. He also suggests that becoming an independent production actually opened rather than closed down opportunities for distribution, business partnerships and marketing – and most importantly the circulation has quadrupled. The figures, margins and staffing numbers are still small in what he calls 'niche magazine publishing' but the model is clearly working and growing slowly, more fully into itself.

PM: How does it differ in presentation from other music monthlies and what would you say it delivers that other music magazines do not?

SB: There aren't many other magazines covering world music, of course. The only competitor in that field is *fRoots* – which has been going twenty-five years. But that's more of a title for committed fans – we're interested in bringing new people to the music. What I think *Songlines* is about is looking at the world through its music – so the writing isn't just about music but about the places and events that make the music. It's cultural politics, economics, ethnicity and so on. That is what other magazines don't deliver, I think, a broader vision. Also I think design and presentation are very much part of making the magazine attractive and accessible – again something which *fRoots* is not. Each issue comes with a free CD of tracks from our Top 10 releases plus a guest playlist from well-known people like Jon Snow in our current issue, or recently Abba's Benny Andersson and writer Philip Pullman.

PM: The covermount CD is unique in the way it blends personal choice with a mix of new releases. How do you make decisions about whom to ask to be the 'editor' of each disc, and, given the very wide range of material included, are the rights/permissions and so on for these CDs difficult to coordinate?

SB: The CD is really important – and is one of the most popular things with our readers. It's very important with world music to be able to get a taste of what it sounds like. Our guest doesn't select the ten 'Top of the World' tracks – they are the best reviewed discs – but we do ask them for five tracks – and yes the permissions are tricky to get, but we do and most people are very happy to grant them. We do get the music out to people who are really interested to hear it.

These apparently populist touches are in fact smart moves that make the magazine and therefore the music more accessible to a much wider audience – an ABBA fan might pick up the issue featuring Benny Andersson's choice – and this is also truthful as Andersson is a leading expert in and practitioner of Swedish folk music. This increases the possibilities of sales for magazine, musician and record company and, in harmony with Broughton's point about cultural politics, makes clear the connections between the apparently obscure and the popular mainstream.

Yet 'freebies' and a bright design constitute only part of what attracts people – what about the rules relating to content?

PM: What are the editorial criteria for inclusion of features and reviews in the magazine?

SB: We will review anything – good and bad – that fits the profile of the magazine. For features we want a story – a new CD release isn't really enough – and a good mix of geographical locations and styles. A story first and good music is what we're interested in.

Broughton's angle on this is effectively that what fits, fits, but at the same time in order to make the critical leap from the small type of the review pages to the full feature then, like any other kind of journalism, 'a story' is required. Yet if *Songlines* seeks to reach out to new audiences alongside informing the insiders how does it organise its distribution?

PM: Bearing in mind the effort you put in to making the magazine approachable to the interested non-expert, how is the magazine distributed in the UK to reach sympathetic, appropriate outlets?

SB: Subscription, the bigger record shops (only HMV now, I think), larger W. H. Smiths. This is one of the main problems – getting people to see the magazine. We have recently started an online digital version – also available on subscription. This is likely to be more and more popular in future I suspect. But we couldn't sustain a free online version.

PM: Picking up the idea of outreach, the magazine has a substantial online presence via the excellent website, podcasts and the like. How important is this to the magazine and can you envisage delivering any part of the magazine as purely online content?

SB: Websites are hugely important these days. They enable people to subscribe and demonstrate what the magazine is like – we have an online digital sampler. We have the free podcast – which has more subscribers than we have to the magazine. It enables people to hear some of the music we're writing about and hopefully direct them to reading the magazine. Our most recent innovation is our iPhone app which gives people easy access to our 'Top of the World' releases, 'Beginners Guides' and enables them to buy tracks.

Songlines has worked hard at connecting itself to the music which is at root the shared interest of both writers and readers. An intriguing aspect of this effort is the Songlines Music Travel company. In this the magazine acknowledges its debt to the early story of world music as a recognisable genre – people travelled to far flung places, heard the music, bought records and tapes and brought them back – and, equally, to the spirit and ethos of the *Rough Guide* travel books, where music sections share space with traditional guidebook facts and figures. I asked Simon Broughton about this enterprise.

PM: I'm very interested by the Songlines Music Travel company and am intrigued to learn how that works, and how decisions are made about where and when to arrange tours? Might I be so bold as to ask how that business is doing and if you have plans for expansion?

SB: Songlines Music Travel is still young (eighteen months) and we're exploring the places and regions that have most potential. The trips are designed for small groups – ten or twelve is about right with a personal, music-oriented tour leader. Most popular seems to be West Africa – we've done two trips to Senegal and one to Mali – which got a fantastic write-up in *The Guardian*. We've done two trips to Cuba – great musical safaris across the island. We've also done shorter trips to Flamenco in Seville, Gnawa music in Morocco, and the wild brass band festival in Guca, Serbia. We're just about breaking even at this point – normal for this sort of business – but the signs are good. It's never going to be large-scale tourism – that's not what this is about. But we do need to spread the word and that's the difficult thing – advertising in travel is extremely expensive so we rely on word of mouth. The great thing is that several people who've been on Songlines Music Travel trips have come back for more.

So while building up this kind of presence, which is made possible by the nature of the music – if we transpose to imagine, say, *Mojo* arranging coach trips to Liverpool or New Orleans, we see that *Songlines* is a different set-up altogether. There is also a growing brand presence within the heart of the industry itself, made manifest in recent years by the title's involvement with the annual UK World Music awards.

PM: How did *Songlines* come to step in when the BBC cancelled the World Music Awards?

SB: We were a partner of the BBC Awards. We could see the importance of the Awards for the artists and the industry which is why we wanted to continue them when the BBC stopped – a money-saving move. And the BBC did spend quite a lot of money on the awards. We couldn't step in with the resources the BBC had, but we did arrange a partnership with WOMAD and an enthusiastic database of voters. We reduced the Awards from seven categories to four to make them more manageable and now we're working to build them up. We had four good winners this year: Rokia Traore (Artist), Amadou & Mariam (Group), Kiran Aluwhalia (Newcomer) and Jah Wobble and the Chinese Dub Orchestra (Cross Cultural Collaboration).

So, like the genesis of the title itself, an absence of provision allowed the title to step in and provide some shape and direction to a difficult, even nebulous genre that needed some correlation and shape put on it. This even without really meaning to, the magazine has become a kind of representative for the whole 'World Music' phenomenon, a kind of textual equivalent to WOMAD and an invaluable mediator for non-Anglophone popular music this world over.

The trade magazine editor: Paul Williams of *Music Week*

In contrast to the other titles regularly published in the UK music market, *Music Week* is a trade paper, serving the music industry. In fact it was the first regular music title I was ever aware of – it was always being read by the faintly frightening proprietor of Project Records in Harehills, Leeds, my local record shop as a child where I bought my first records, purchases funded by paper-round and dog-walking money. The thought that there was a weekly publication about records intrigued me and one Saturday morning – it was always a Saturday when I visited the shop – I dared myself to ask for a look. He lobbed the paper over the counter. I was perplexed but fascinated by the out-lines of promotional campaigns, news of forthcoming releases, heavily discounted offers on new acts and charts, charts, charts. The most remarkable thing to an eleven year old was the detail and planning of the promotional campaign – I remember that this issue featured a splash on promoting a band called Slik featuring a very young Midge Ure who later fronted Ultravox and was a major force behind the Band Aid and Live Aid projects. This was a great surprise as I had imagined, if I had thought about it all, that success was a happy accident and meritocratic to a fault – these must be the best records, mustn't they? That's why they are successful! Looking at that long-gone issue of *Music Week* started the scales falling from my eyes.

The magazine was launched in 1959 as *Record Retailer*, a somewhat belated response to the explosion in demand for the new music; it became *Music Week* in 1972, then demonstrated a sensitivity to changing markets (and the title's survival) by briefly becoming *Music and Video Week* in 1981 until *Video Week* was launched as a separate title in 1983. *Video Week* has long gone; *Music Week* persists. The magazine established a connection with the history of consumer rather than retailer publishing when it 'absorbed' the weekly *Record Mirror* on the latter's 1991 demise as a stand-alone title. What sets it apart from the other titles we look at here is that it serves the industry, rather than the client, the producer rather than the consumer. It is always an eye-opening read.

I spoke to *Music Week*'s editor, Paul Williams and asked him how he saw the magazine's position in relation to the rest of the commercial music magazine market in the UK as well as the music industry in the wider sense.

> *PM:* Do you think that *Music Week* has an overlap with other sections of the UK music press?
>
> *PW:* Well, there have been more overlaps in the last ten years or so, as there has been more interest in the industry, because of the difficulties therein post-Napster – the EMI saga has featured very strongly in the financial pages of the mainstream news media. Likewise, in a magazine like *Q* you are more likely to get a story about the industry, partly due to an increased awareness of how the industry works among the readership and also because it impacts not least upon earnings for artists. The shows such as X-Factor have some influence too; the 'back end' of the industry has come into the light, making it more obvious how the process works – consequently readers feel closer to the process and don't feel the dissociation that they might have once felt from the 'business' dimension, so are happier to read about this element of the industry – the 'industrial' part of the industry, rather than reading about the artists and their lives and so on, the old interview/promotional model.

So the implication here is that there is a wider and more general sense of how the industry works and an acknowledgement that the music will be promoted like any other expensively assembled product. The machinations of the industry are now a given as part of the way that music is mediated and sold.

> *PM:* This is different of course from the sort of thing that the original *Smash Hits* forced to an endpoint and logical conclusion – the 'what colour are your socks' line of questioning, where the business dimension was simply ignored.
>
> *PW:* Yes, it is quite different from that – although those guys were the biggest business men of the lot of course! But *Music Week* is

still different from the consumer press, I'd say, in both content and relationship to the industry – it's a kind of trust thing. We have access to the movers and shakers as it were. I think of *Music Week* as a kind of local newspaper or village pump, in that the people you write about are the ones who are going to read it, be they people already in the industry or those aspiring to be involved in a way which goes beyond wanting to be in a band. That goes for the established reader and the newcomer, be they musician or music students looking to understand the industry better. *Music Week*'s core audience has become smaller but the make-up of that audience is more complicated than it was. Fifteen years ago we were more about what record companies were doing, who was being groomed and launched or repackaged and so on, but now we extend far beyond the record labels, into more disciplines such as the whole live field, music publishing and of course digital.

This assessment of the magazine's role as 'village pump' for the industry is an apposite one; this is in stark contrast to the consumer magazines where we would not necessarily expect the subjects of the articles to also be avid readers of them. The strength of the publication comes in part from knowing precisely who their readership is – this is partly because the great majority of readers of the magazine are also subscribers rather than picking it up anonymously from a newsagent's shelf – but also because of this ability to mediate the news of the industry back to itself – like a local newspaper, in fact. The magazine has, he feels, been able to free itself from concerning itself only with industry fashions or rivalries, dealing instead with wider and more fundamental topics for the industry ('live music, publishing and digital'), in a period of swift change and great uncertainty for that industry. Williams' reference to the 'movers and shakers' of the industry involves both the independent record shop owner and the Head of Marketing at EMI, both of whom are links in the chain. Indeed their fates are bound together regarding the success or failure of any given project, be that an individual artist who has received heavy investment or a brand new format for selling the music.

I wondered how the advent of 'self-marketing' and purely independent music production distributed online, often for free, had impacted upon how the magazine deals with the selling of music.

>   *PW*:   Well one thing I'd say is that the power in the business is now with the artist. Artists and management have interest and

stakes in different sectors, but the music provides the common
factor of course, and companies don't dictate touring/publishing
or sponsorships in the way they did.

PM: By the artist do you mean Radiohead or Paul McCartney not
liking the regime at EMI, or the kid putting their demos onto
MySpace?

PW: Well, the Radiohead thing got lots of mainstream press but
I'm not sure if you look at it how much control they really do
have . . . but it's true that the artist is no longer at the beck and
call of the record company in the way that they were twenty years
ago – they aren't told what to issue or with whom they have to
register the publishing, and the consumer has more control over
access – whereas formerly it was record or tape and that was that.
Now there are so many ways – and it's not just music that's like
this, I'd include films, sport and TV too – there is much more
control over the product for the producer and for the consumer.
Music Week has to reflect all of these changes while still acknowledging that the music industry still exists and is struggling to
accommodate all these changes.

Here Williams makes the point that the route from producer to
consumer is still strong but now is able to be much more direct – in
some ways circumventing the very people and businesses that *Music
Week* addresses – and so the magazine, which functions as both voice
and observer of the British music retail industry, seeks to defend the
interests of that industry while also getting to grips with the wider and
very powerful changes that the whole entertainment sector is undergo-
ing. I wondered, in that case, whether the magazine saw itself simply
as reporting on what is happening or whether, as the 'voice' or local
newspaper of the British music retail industry, it felt the responsibility to actually campaign and engage in discussion in defence of that
industry.

PM: Given these new conditions, would you say a publication like
Music Week needs to be 'reflective' or 'directive', that is a reporting or a campaigning voice?

PW: Good question. It's important that *Music Week* is informa-
tive, but we are also a campaigning paper, two examples being
the arguments surrounding copyright extension. So we've been
asking, should there be copyright extension, and if so, how should
it work? We've been saying that yes there should be extension,
and the arguments we've used have been taken up at a higher

level and put before the government, so *Music Week* saying 'yes' to this issue has helped get the idea back on track. Likewise P2P [peer-to-peer file sharing on the Internet], I wrote an article in favour of legislation after Peter Mandelson suggested that tougher action should be taken against serial file-sharers, and this was used by the industry again at higher levels in government in order to bolster this case. Ben Bradshaw [then Secretary of State for Culture, Media and Sport in the British government] has a piece in the current issue of *Music Week* (September 2009) partly as a response to this kind of article – we are keeping the debate going.

So the magazine seeks to fulfil its remit as mouthpiece for the anxieties and concerns of the music retail business as much as it continues to function as a mediating platform for advertising and promotional campaigns. Indeed, as Williams's comments here show, *Music Week* has been a leader in ensuring that debates surrounding the digital revolution are not set aside or misunderstood. Using the new technologies of mediation and communication are important for this too of course, and in common with the consumer titles *Music Week* has worked hard at developing a substantive web presence. I asked Paul Williams what role he expected the website to take and what contribution it might make to the future of the title.

> *PW*:   I'd anticipate the magazine and the website to have more distinctive identities over time – the magazine will always be about analysis, features and context where the website is more firmly focused on breaking news. The subscribers are more likely to be the core readership, that is the people already working within the industry or with a very active interest in the business, where the web users might just be researching a single topic or want a little more detail about a current idea or news item. Very different audiences, in other words.
>
> We are, however, about to announce a stand-alone digital edition of the magazine for subscription purposes – at present, buying a sub for the magazine gets you full access to the website and a digital version of the magazine delivered via e-mail once a week. As for the future – my hunch is that there will be a mixture going forward, as print offers something online doesn't especially for longer features and so on, where online is better for access on the move and the quick update/reminder. Of course we are all wondering whether the future will need to be

free online content, after the *Guardian* model, or the Rupert Murdoch approach of getting people to pay . . . after all twenty years ago if you'd asked people to pay over and above the TV licence people would have said 'Why? I already get the four channels, why would I want to pay for more?' So the future must be offering something that the customer feels is worth the extra, so that they say, 'yes, I'm happy to pay for that'. Whether that is exclusive content or something yet to be discovered we'll have to see. But *Music Week* is certainly in a position to explore these possibilities.

In these terms, the magazine seems to anticipate a bright future in which the online and print editions are in collusion rather than competition – as he coolly notes, print can deliver something online cannot and vice versa. Together these formats make for a stronger, readily accessible and more widely read publication. Over and above the payments required – *Music Week* retails for the relatively high price of £5.95 – the 'exclusive content or something yet to be discovered' must be sufficiently tempting to make the extra investment worthwhile. That openness to the thing that is yet to be discovered characterises the magazine over its history, with its adaptability and swiftness to respond to changes in the industry – such as the conversion to video and then the dropping of it again after that market was superseded. In this the magazine certainly is, as Williams claims, the local newspaper, reporting and campaigning and presenting the concerns of the community in the best and most adaptable way it can. It is a key mediator of the way music is presented, sold and understood either in the local record shop, the boardrooms of EMI or the indie label, or within the offices of state.

Exercise questions

1. Look at one monthly pop magazine, one specialist 'niche' magazine, one daily broadsheet and one tabloid. Analyse the popular music content. How does the writing differ across these four types of publication?
2. What is foregrounded as being relevant and significant information ? What does this say about (a) the publication; (b) the musical genre involved; and (c) the publication's assumptions about its imagined audience? What are the supposed relevant knowledge levels? Are these well-known narratives or are they fully explained and contextualised?

3. Is the music writer necessarily a 'cultural gatekeeper'?
4. What might be the advantage of an online blog or publication over the monthly magazine ? Which would you rather read and why?

2 'Everybody's on *Top of the Pops*': Popular Music on Television

Pop on British TV is a curious case study, indexing the rising, falling and passing of musical styles, trends and fads but also the changing nature of TV itself – how it feels it necessary to portray, display and contextualise the music. There is also the issue of public broadcasting as opposed to commercial enterprise. This is in itself akin to the bargain that is required to be struck by all musicians as they engage with the machinations of the music industry – that is the trade-off between the art and the commerce. TV has mixed responsibilities toward pop – to simply show that which is popular as well as to provide, as Mark Cooper, producer of *Later* and Creative Head of Music Entertainment at the BBC, told me, 'the idea of curating, and creating an aesthetic'.

The field of pop on television, unlike music on film, is curiously underwritten. In the early 1990s there was a run of material such as Goodwin (1993) and Frith and Goodwin (1994) responding to the rise of MTV and the music video as a media text, but it was some time before Austerlitz (2008) and Railton and Watson (2011) turned to the topic again. Books on music as created television spectacle beyond videos and MTV are puzzlingly rare; Mundy (1999) and Inglis (2010) offered wider views of the connection between music and the small screen but there has been no definitive work in the field as yet. Even the iconic pop TV show *Top of the Pops* (BBC 1964–2006) has yet to be written about in depth. Instead the story has come via memoir and autobiography from, for example, Nightingale (1999), Harris (2001) and Kershaw (2011), all former presenters of the BBC's 'serious' music show of the 1970s and 1980s, the *Old Grey Whistle Test* (see Mills, in Inglis 2010). After that show was cancelled in 1987 the BBC's music coverage became diffuse and dispersed for some years.

This was the place at which my discussion with Mark Cooper began. He has been producer of BBC2's *Later . . . With Jools Holland* since the show began in 1992 and is currently also Creative Head of Music Entertainment at the BBC as well as being responsible for the coverage of outside broadcast events such as the Glastonbury Festival.

> *PM*:   There was a substantial gap between the close of the *Whistle Test* and the arrival of *Later* – what in your view was the BBC's policy on putting music on screen in that period?
>
> *MC*:   Well this was before my time but it was Janet Street-Porter who came in and ended the *Old Grey Whistle Test*, and it was the era of *Def II*, Normski and the only show in that period I can recall was called *Snub*, made by Brenda Kelly. It was indie, so the Jesus and Mary Chain, the Fall and so on . . . not that many episodes, but enough . . . at the time I think music was seen as niche genres so it was *Dance Energy* and it was *Snub*. Neither were 'live in the studio' though in that sense. So I remember when the *Late Show* started which I worked on from 1990 [it started in 1989] there was a sense that live music should be part of the agenda of the programme, almost precisely because that was missing from the BBC's output.

Here we see how influential the coming and going of producers can be within a broadcaster's output, even one the size of the BBC – Janet Street-Porter was brought into the BBC on the strength of her Network 7 'strand' on Channel 4, a kind of channel within a channel, which sought to replace *The Tube*. The *DEF II* strand on BBC2 (1988–94) sought to recreate that kind of model and, indeed, success. It was perhaps less successful than her employers' anticipated, with the modish quick cutting and high-speed turnover of topics working against a focus on music as music rather than as a backdrop to a lifestyle. So it was left to a more traditional kind of arts programming on *The Late Show*, a format which stretches back to the 1960s arts strand *Late Night Line Up* in the BBC tradition, to offer a more open space for music to be seen and heard. Out of this five-night a week arts magazine format which would often focus on music sprang *Later . . . With Jools Holland*, Holland having proved himself on Channel 4's *The Tube* (1982–7).

> *PM*:   How did *Later . . . With Jools Holland* evolve out of the *Late Show* strand?
>
> *MC*:   Well there was a lot of downtime in the *Late Show* studio; the *LS* was on four nights a week and it had its own studio and quite often a lot of the programmes would consist largely of VT [video

tape] films. Most of the people who worked on the *Late Show* wanted to make films, and fewer studio-oriented producers, so it was something that Michael Jackson [then editor of *The Late Show*] and I discussed . . . from when I joined the show in January 1990, I was straight away enjoying putting on loads of different kinds of music, and as much as possible, and ranging across as many genres as possible – The Kronos Quartet to Ice-T, Julee Cruise to Cowboy Junkies. So there was this great studio space, the directors liked it and it was great having that element in the programme, and so after a year or so Michael Jackson and I were discussing, and wondered could you do a music show and pilot it in that space – for not much money! The idea was intrinsically that it would be journalistic and going into lots of different genres, to take the best of each world and feature them next to each other.

For the first series, we had to record it in the studio before *The Late Show* started – we had to be out of there by 10 o'clock, as it was on air at 11.15, and then we'd edit what we had and put it out after *TLS* at about 12, 12.30 time – it was completely terrifying! Fundamentally the idea was to deliver live music, to be cross-genre, and for it all to be in the room at the same time; everything happened in real time, in one room in one shot. It couldn't lie. I'd worked on *The Word* [1990–5] on Channel 4 – they had a lot of shows after *The Tube* closed, and they shot bands for *The Word* in Pinewood and it was an international show and I was very aware of the pressure on the bookers to get names, in order to get ratings, and afterwards I wanted to try to put a show together where it would maintain a level of excellence, and it would be good just because it was good rather than chasing the latest thing. That was the philosophy.

So, as with the arrival of Janet Street-Porter signalling the end of one phase of BBC music programming, Mark Cooper's involvement with *The Late Show* brought about another shift, this time one which unashamedly foregrounded the music as worthy of airtime in and of itself – 'that was the philosophy'. His pathway to BBC2 was in fact the same as that of Street-Porter – coming in from the supposedly less constrained environment of Channel 4 (although here he remembers the 'pressure on the bookers to get names' on *The Word*) to the more formalised and disciplined context of BBC2. *Later . . . With Jools Holland* had from its inception a natural and unforced balance between content and presentation – the audience are relaxed but know that the show is about the music, not about them – or indeed, despite the nomenclature, about the host particularly.

I asked Mark Cooper about the role of the host:

PM: What in your view is the role of the presenter in pop TV? How does Jools Holland conform to or deviate from that model as far as his contribution to *Later* goes?

MC: Jools isn't a journalist or a DJ so that in itself is unusual – *Top of the Pops* presenters were usually DJs migrating from Radio 1, and on the *OGWT* there was the tradition of getting journalists in – essentially their tone was journalistic. Or it was Bob Harris. Bob was predominantly a tone, I think, a very knowledgeable tone, but a tone nonetheless. Jools isn't either of those things; he's a musician first and foremost. Musically Jools is a small-c conservative, he loves where music comes from, and after *The Tube* he'd got rid of the urge to be a naughty boy, and was much more open to the wider world of music, a much more inclusive philosophy. Which isn't to say he's not interested in new music, because he is, but he's a student of the Beatles, the Rolling Stones and all points back from there. He has enthusiasm, and the trust of musicians, because he's a great player and has a track record. As for choosing him to front the show, it wasn't as conscious as this makes it sound, but he had done TV, he had charm, and he has proved himself the ringmaster – we always conceived of *Later* as a *show* – so if *OGWT* was a magazine that bands performed on, we saw *Later* as a musical narrative that would unfold over an hour. As an MC, Jools 'brought the show', and when he plays with people or talks to them, he speaks their language . . . he gets some flak from journalists for the way he interviews people as you get an encounter which is musical, not journalistic . . . however, it gets material out of people that is often unusual.

Here Cooper places both host and show in a line of continuity within the representation of music on British television. If Holland 'brings the show' then his role is indeed different from the *Top of the Pops* host whose job was in some ways a very simple one – to provide a link between what we had seen and what we were about to see. The *Old Grey Whistle Test* presenter, on the other hand, was obliged to mediate and contextualise via that show's magazine format. Holland is on a level with the guests, like the *TOTP* host, but is also on a par with the musicians due to his own impressive career with Squeeze and his solo work. As with an *OGWT* host, he is a trusted figure, a cultural gatekeeper of a kind, but the difference is that he has thus far never subjected an act to the treatment Bob Harris meted out to the New York Dolls when he called them 'mock rock' in 1974, or the tart remarks directed toward the handful of punk acts which made it onto the show before his departure in early 1978 (see Mills 2010). Tellingly Cooper observes that Holland gets flak from journalists for his interviewing style, probably because of his 'insider' status or, as Cooper puts it, 'he speaks their language'. This lends the programme both authority and ease.

Yet the show is not simply the dynamic between the host and the music; the studio environment is equally important. The bright and direct sets for *Top of the Pops* provided a perfect showcase for the music, as did the sober environs of 'Pres B', the small weather forecast studio used for the early days of the *Old Grey Whistle Test*. Likewise, the floor-level views and stars in the audience format of *Ready Steady Go!* (ITV 1964–6) partly informed the benign chaos of *The Tube* and this in its turn influenced the performance and audience spaces found on *Later*. Mark Cooper observed that there was definite design at work here:

> MC: We wanted to get as much music in the room as possible. Most music shows have the audiences in front of the band, which always seemed a bit third hand, so we have this single vantage point, with the cameras in front of the group so we have this direct relationship with the audience at home. We wanted to use every corner of the room, and the whole purpose of the room is the contrasts really. Also we couldn't afford to have stages, and a practical response to having an empty studio, and wondering how much music we could get into it; putting them round the walls seemed the best way to get the most in. That leaves the place in the middle of the floor for the host and around the piano, and so the cameras and so on are free to sweep around. We shot it inside out, with the cameras in the middle, shooting out to the edges, with the audience behind the bands. We wanted the audience at home to feel that the show was for them, predominantly.

Like the signature look of the *OGWT*, borne out of the tiny studio they were obliged to use, the lack of stages in the studio has given *Later* part of its on-screen character. Likewise, the decision to make the event 'in the round' has placed the viewer's eye, via the camera, right at the centre of the proceedings. Furthermore, the space is wholly democratic; part of the show's strength lies in its equivalence and even-handed presentation, with the circular studio placing established acts and new faces cheek by jowl, all encouraged to join in the jam at the show's opening. But how do the acts get there? On *Top of the Pops*, an act was on-screen because their song was, right at that moment, genuinely popular – a point proved by their position in the 'stock market for your hi-fi', the Top 40, and the programme's policy of only playing songs that were climbing the chart or were the number one: *Later* is not subject to such rapid rhythms of approval. The *Old Grey Whistle Test* had a selection policy based on the views of producer Mike Appleton and the show's presenters, notably Bob Harris; is it the same for *Later*?

> *PM*: What are the criteria for inclusion on *Later*? Have they changed over the years?
>
> *MC*: The idea of each show is to build a magazine, really . . . partly it's who is available that week, and it's partly about . . . responsibility, I suppose, not wanting to have an imbalance. We had a show this year [3/6 November 2009, episode 8 series 35] where they were all 'names', we had the Foo Fighters, Norah Jones and Jay-Z, so for the same show we booked Stornaway, who were unsigned at the time, and Erik Mongrain, an obscure Canadian guitar player to balance it out. So we see it in a fairly missionary way, in the Peel/BBC tradition of wanting to spread the word about something new. So if the show turns too far any which way (commercial, obscure, mainstream, avant garde) we'll try and pull it back in. The elements should contrast. It's an illusion anyway that more people will watch because it has the big names . . . the integrity of the show is important, so people come to it not necessarily knowing every name on the bill but knowing that it will all be good. The audience is very loyal to *Later* and that's what they like, I think. The idea I suppose is to build an aesthetic of taste which will be durable and long-lasting and meet that public service ethos. In fact I think that's why the show has lasted so long; not just because of the mix or how we do it or that technically the sound engineers ensure it always sounds so good, but that it is close to the DNA of what the BBC is for. Like on the Peel Show, you try and build up a trust with the audience. That's something you're constantly adjusting, or getting wrong, but always wanting to do right.

This emphasis on balance might, we feel, fit with the BBC ideal ('what the BBC is for') but what is also significant here is the preservation of the show as something other than a promotional star vehicle – 'the integrity of the show' – the democracy of the studio space and set-up extends to the booking policy too. Thus this becomes part of the value of the show to its core audience. Just as important is the assertion that the elements should contrast, so that there is no musical 'identity' to which the show can be lashed – it is not a rock show, nor is it a blues, indie, folk or country show, yet all of these styles may well be heard within a single hour's programming. Interestingly, Mark Cooper cites as a model not a previous TV show but a radio programme – the John Peel show which ran on BBC Radio 1 for twenty-seven years and certainly built up a trust with an audience. The BBC has tried hard but, at the time of writing, has failed to find a replacement for Peel and it may well be the case that *Later* is the closest thing to the spirit of his shows that the BBC has.

Cooper does not mention the role of host, but it is one which is clearly key to a show's identity and success. Jools Holland functions well as an MC, a convention with which we are familiar, but is unusual in that he occasionally makes musical contributions via the piano, the instrument with which he is synonymous. Within the format of *Later*, the piano is the symbol of its musicality and also Holland's right to work as mediator on behalf of the audience – he knows that of which he speaks, and his status as a respected equal to the guests is embodied by the on-screen presence of the piano. Interviews with musicians are frequently conducted at the piano while producers or other guests are met at one of the small tables which dot the perimeter of the 'stage' area. These provide a pleasing and relaxed 'cafe culture' ambience but also function as a kind of discrete barrier, marking the distinction between the performers and the studio audience. As Cooper notes, the visual spectacle is predominantly constructed for the audience at home – it is after all a television programme rather than a televised event – and the camera eye is at the centre of all, providing the kind of access that the studio audience cannot get. However, Mark Cooper also told me of how those two audiences are sometimes brought together.

PM: Have you ever been tempted to include archive features, comedy or more 'magazine'-style elements into the show?
MC: Not really, it's a hard format to change because it's about the reality of the room and as soon as you go away from the room it's like you're diminishing it a bit. The room has its own energy, which comes from the contrast between the bodies in it, the bands – so every time you go away from it, you lose some of that energy. Why would you fill a room with all that and then leave it behind, y'know? It's not that we haven't thought about it but it's

how would you do that? We sometimes use archive clips in interviews but it's always to the room . . . we always figure if it's good
in the room, it'll be good to watch. In the end, if we introduced
those other materials it would be another show, I suppose.

The show's home audience values these moments of connection,
often underlined by cuts to shots of Holland and guests watching the
archive clip playing on a monitor or the studio audience watching
a larger screen. This can prove unexpectedly interesting and often
quite moving, such as a November 2009 show in which Roger Taylor
of Queen watched film of his younger self and band mates, his face
betraying both delight and melancholy. Cooper's description of the
energy in the room is akin to that of organic, living thing that keeps
the show moving forward and he is indeed loath to leave that behind.
As he says, to do so would be 'another show', and not the one that succeeds as *Later*.

Building on that sustained success, on 31 March 2008 *Later* went
'live'. This was not the first time they had done this – I was at a show
broadcast live to air at Pennington's nightclub in Bradford on Friday,
25 May 2001, the only time the show has been taken 'on the road' and
produced outside the usual BBC studios at White City. From 2008,
however, the show took a bold step forward in terms of format and
presentation – the live show is broadcast on BBC2 at 10–10.30 p.m.
on a Tuesday, and then an hour-long recorded version is broadcast
on the Friday of the same week. Importantly, the two shows are quite
different entities – the longer show is not simply an edit of the live half
hour. Mark Cooper told me why the decision had been taken to renew
the show's format in this way:

PM: Why did the show go 'live' in 2008?

MC: Well really because they had to find a way of *Later* playing
in peak because the amount of money it costs to play as late as it
does, at 11.30 . . . it's expensive for an 11.30 show! The idea was
how can we get more 'value' out of it . . . so could we do a half
hour at 10 p.m., and the idea being that it was both live but then
also a longer, recorded show with more material in it in the usual
Friday slot. Wouldn't that be great to return to the live to air
element that had been missing? So it was a real opportunity, but
exhausting . . . the first series was very stressful because we were
trying to do two shows in a night, the Friday night first and then
we turn around and do the live show. It's difficult because we've
already got a lot to deal with . . . it's like a mini rock festival in the

room, and to achieve all that technically and get your head round it, it's tricky! But now we've been doing it for this long it's much easier and we really love it, Jools and the artists find it really rewarding, and there's a buzz and an edge that comes from doing it live that you just can't really replace, and it raises everybody's game.

Here we see how that basic economic realities of putting music on television can be brought to bear upon the format. The cheap option of miming or the middle ground of 'pre-records', as was sometimes practised by *Top of the Pops*, is not available to the show – indeed *Later* is marked out as unique by its insistence upon 'liveness' as even the *Old Grey Whistle Test*, despite its reputation for always being played live, did, in its early days, feature some lip-synched performances: 'Just like *TOTP!*' remembered original host Richard Williams (see Mills 2010). The sheer hard work involved and the nerve-jangling nature of the task is clear from Cooper's observations here – 'very stressful . . . it's difficult because we've already got a lot to deal with . . . like a mini rock festival . . . it's tricky!'– yet the advantages seem to outweigh the difficulties by some way, once the new format was settled in. The 'buzz' and 'edge' that live broadcast brings takes the programme, and the viewer, closer once again to the experience of being 'in the room' at a live event rather than a mediated television show. Which of course it is, but some of the breathlessness of the 'liveness' of Mark Cooper's imagined 'mini rock festival' blows through the programme.

PM: What impact has the division into 'live ' and 'recorded' editions had on the way you make the show?

MC: It's made it slicker I suppose; we have to start at 8.30 and we have to finish by 9.50 at the very latest, and then the live show starts at 10. It's pretty close to time. We vary probably four or five songs in that time over the two shows . . . there's quite a bit of difference between the two shows if you look at them together, in terms of running order and so on, songs often differ too. It's enabled us to get more songs out there, actually, and more contrast which is what we're always after. The Friday show is deeper and richer – more artists, more songs – and is also more for the committed fans; the Tuesday show is seen by more people who aren't committed fans, and are just grazing if they don't want the news, you know. Tuesday reaches a broader audience. It's a slightly weird time to be on, if you look across television schedules, there's nothing quite like it anywhere at that time and on that day!

Traditionally, non-chart music shows have been on Friday, either early evening [*The Tube* etc.] or late night [*Later* itself], a sort of here comes the weekend thing . . . the *Whistle Test* was on midweek [usually Tuesdays] but that was more of a magazine, so here's this weird beast that's all music for half an hour . . . it's quite hard getting the dynamic right at 10 o'clock. It's different, it's more compressed and 'comin'' at ya' in a way; it's hectic and sometimes hard to tell if it's too long or too short, so pieces suddenly seem really long, or you think 'I want more of that'. So I think we're still trying to learn what *Later* at 10 o'clock would be . . . if you'd started off the other way round, inventing a music show to play on Tuesday at 10, you wouldn't have done it that way! We've done it in reverse, really, building a Friday show and then thinking how you can distil that to go out at 10 on a Tuesday. You would maybe have come up with something 'magazine', more like the *Whistle Test* I guess . . . but how could you do that with a room full of musicians straining at the leash?

How indeed? The quick 'hit' of the live Tuesday show draws some of its strength from it not being like anything else across the evening's stranding, as Mark Cooper notes here.

So, for example, the episode of *Later* broadcast on 17 November 2009 featured David Gray, Corinne Bailey Rae, the Decemberists, Rox and Big Pink. The recorded show screened on 20 November featured all these adding in the Low Anthem and the Stan Treacy Quartet. The musical mix that Mark Cooper speaks of is demonstrably at work here: British, American, established, brand new, quiet, loud, jazz, indie, AOR – you choose the category. This is the 'weird beast' that Cooper describes being bold enough – and trusting enough of its audience – to present these juxtapositions. Some of the traditional signifiers of distinction within televised musical performance are absent from the show – for example, the lighting is evenly shared across the acts; there are no spectacular light shows or 'imported' choreography of light and colour from the acts' standard live shows. The democratic space offered by the show requires that the million-seller and the new signing are presented as equals. These are the aesthetic criteria – there are of course practical concerns, such as, in the 'Live' show, the plain fact of the need to fit everything into thirty minutes.

In all of this we see how *Later . . . With Jools Holland* draws together, and draws upon, many of the extant models of presenting and representing popular music on television – it has the liveness which most obviously, through its host, connects it to *The Tube*, and even further back to Jack Good's daring *Oh Boy!* In its mix of what is deemed 'good' and what is genuinely popular it is connected to shows like the *Old Grey Whistle Test* while in its key role for the good-humoured, enthusiastic audience it even draws upon the audio-visual traditions of *Top of the Pops* and *Ready Steady Go!*. Yet it bears equally traces of a connoisseurial tradition, what Mark Cooper calls the 'curating' element which connects it again to the *Old Grey Whistle Test* and a separate history of music documentary. Yet, paradoxically, it is the sound as much as the look of the show which makes the programme as successful and as well-regarded as it is. Most of all it is the musicality of the space that it offers on British television that makes it such a potent blend of all these extant models into a long-running format which is always fresh because the music is always fresh. Thus the music and its visual representation is in a kind of accord and a harmonious unity which lends the show its feel of being entirely natural and unforced in its presentation of popular music on television.

TV exercises

1. Does pop depend upon its visualisation on TV in order to be successful?
2. Is the mediation of live music on TV different to that in a hall, theatre or festival?
3. Select a single week or look at a TV listings magazine. Analyse the schedule for music output: what kind of presentation do you find? Is it live music? Documentaries? Music video?
4. Why do you think music tends to be concentrated on dedicated channels rather than spread evenly across terrestrial schedules?

3 Sold on Song? The Use of Music in Television Advertising

The relationship between popular song and advertising is a very old one – indeed it has its roots in the cries you'll hear at any market in any town in any country in the world. The stallholders shout out, trying to get your attention, seeking an advantage in the marketplace. These 'cries' are the antecedents of the advertising jingle, which in turn was the first overt offspring of the relationship between music and commerce, long before mediation, be it printing or recording, made a song into a commodity that could itself be taken to market. Such searching for an edge in a crowded marketplace taps into the emotional impact of a melody, of course, no matter how brief or slight. Indeed the writing of a jingle is in itself a craft not easily mastered or cultivated – if a television theme needs a kind of discipline to bring it in at exactly one minute then the composition of a jingle needs to be mindful of time, purpose and the products. Early jingles were little tunes sung outside stores or a politician's rallies – Joel Coen's *O Brother Where Art Thou?* shows an example of this – and businesses would employ musicians to play jingles but also to represent the firm. For example, the Huntley & Palmers biscuit factory in Reading, Berkshire, had a string quartet which would give performances of 'real' music in the town and play little 'jingles' advertising the firm's products, connecting the two types of song. The archives of the band, including recordings, are held in the Huntley & Palmers Collection at the University of Reading.

The sponsorship of an arts wing was good for a company's reputation as an enlightened employer and contributor to the community. Such bands would play popular tunes of the day, mixing in the 'jingles' so that the product became associated, by stealthy proximity, with the hit tunes of the day. 'Lucky Strike', the American cigarette brand, was a pioneer in this, beginning the *Lucky Strike Music Hour* on US country-wide radio in 1928 featuring commercials and appearances by stars of the day such as Frank Sinatra. Lucky Strike became associated with the new idea of a competitive 'chart rundown' in the show *Your Hit Parade* which began in 1935. Thus the very idea of music as a competitive field stems in part from this kind of contact with advertising.

There has been much writing about advertising, notably Tungate (2007) and Fletcher (2008), and in connection with specific products such as Coca-Cola (Pendergrast 2000; Hays 2007), but surprisingly little about the use of music in advertising. Klein (2010) addresses aspects of the topic and Petrusich (2007) included a little section on the furore that surrounded Volkswagen's use of Nick Drake's 'Pink Moon', but most writing about music and ads has been confined to trade papers, as an accepted and unquestioned part of the package of signifiers which help a product sell. Yet, we might feel, the licensing of a piece of music is risky for an artist – what might it do to their reputation? How will their extant audience react? Will the client consider the ad a failure, thus denting hopes of further licensing? A song like James Brown's 'I Feel Good' has been licensed for use in ads for over forty separate products, and the Dandy Warhols' 'Bohemian Like You' seems to be catching it up – in both cases, it was good news for the act's finances and reputation. Perhaps the most famous and most actively pursued case in recent years was Moby's licensing of every track on his hit album *Play* to advertisers. This was a reverse of the usual policy of caution and caginess on the part of the artist and as such was in itself a kind of art statement – this music was for sale so why not sell it? Yet it also ensured that the music would be heard, and according to *Wired* magazine, the songs on *Play* were 'sold hundreds of times . . . a licensing venture so staggeringly lucrative that the album was a financial success months before it reached its multi-platinum sales total' (see Miller 2008).

Yet this marriage between music and advertising is not always so harmonious. As noted, the use of Nick Drake's song 'Pink Moon' on a Volkswagen ad caused great consternation (see 2007) and Northern Soul connoisseurs raged when Kentucky Fried Chicken ads used some of their most revered tunes to sell fast food. Bob Dylan's licensing of his song 'Lovesick' to advertisers of Victoria's Secret lingerie caused a similar flurry of comment – 'Talk about Judas', fumed *The Independent* (7 April 2004) although, interestingly, a subsequent use of 'Blowin' in the Wind' in a UK advert for the Co-operative supermarket chain passed almost unremarked upon in comparison: on 27 January 2009 trade publication *Talking Retail* reported it thus:

Bob Dylan has given the Co-operative Group (Co-op) permission to use one of his songs in a television commercial, the retailer said today. The singer-songwriter's 'Blowin' in the Wind' will be used in a new Co-op campaign that begins next month. Columbia Records

UK managing director Mike Smith said: 'It is rare for Bob Dylan to license his recordings to TV ads. The decision to do so with the Co-op and 'Blowin' in the Wind' shows a willingness to embrace fresh ways of reaching a new audience through an ethical and fair-trade organisation.

Co-op director of marketing Patrick Allen added: 'We have invested heavily in the re-branding exercise and now through Dylan's iconic track we can tell everyone about the new look Co-operative.' The adverts come at the end of a two-year programme in which the Co-op has re-branded its entire operation.

Here we see both the internal and external logic for matching the song to the product – in this case not a single item at all, but a whole organisation being represented by the unimpeachable values of a song like 'Blowin' in the Wind', and also, for Columbia as well as Dylan, the logic of 'a willingness to embrace fresh ways of reaching a new audience through an ethical and fair-trade organisation'. The meaning of the song is in some ways fixed, but this does not mean it cannot change – the song's lyric is a series of open questions, unanswered and unanswerable in any conventional sense. This makes it a perfect choice for 'an ethical and fair-trade organisation' and was an important factor in changing the way the Co-op was seen as it rebranded itself. The song risks a kind of associative branding in itself, of course, but the song was already a kind of metatext (partly why it was chosen, perhaps) and the 'borrowed interest' flows from the song to the brand and less so the other way: the song survives.

The problems as well as the advantages offered by having someone like Dylan or Lennon in an ad – or even simply appearing to have their endorsement – are illustrated by the controversy surrounding a 'fake' Lennon voiceover used in an ad for the Citroën DS3 car in 2008. A film clip of Lennon, in what seems to be a late 1960s interview, had its audio removed and replaced with the voice of an actor mimicking his voice, talking about refusing the lure of nostalgia, which dovetails into the strapline 'Anti-Retro'. The visuals were manipulated by 'CGI' to make it appear as if he were speaking the words. This blatant deception was, amazingly, sanctioned by the Lennon estate, and his son Sean took substantial flak for defending it. Lennon was also 'impersonated' for a charity advert seeking to distribute laptops to children as if they were bread and water. This clearly illustrates the cultural capital and high levels of borrowed interest that a piece of music or a musician can deliver to an advert and, thereby, the product in question, even if it is merely the ghost of a suggestion of endorsement.

I spoke to Jeremy Lascelles about how music is used in advertising and on television. He is currently chief executive officer (CEO) of Chrysalis music and has a long and distinguished history in the music industry, having worked his way up through retail and artist and repertoire at Virgin, launching his own record label, Offside, before becoming one of the leading lights in the developing connection between popular music and advertising.

PM: What are the processes via which a song becomes attached to or used in a visual text such as an advert, a television programme or a film?

JL: A multitude of different ways! I could give you a very long answer! But in essence you've got the creative hand behind matching the music to the visual event. At an advertising agency you have 'the creatives' who put together a format. It's their responsibility to source music – for a film, you'll have a music supervisor who again is charged with putting all the music into that project; on TV it's the same, with a slightly scaled down version so you have someone in-house across the channel. At the BBC they tend to have specialists in different musical fields.

PM: So you have someone sorting the music for *Ashes to Ashes*, and someone for *Poirot*, say?

JL: Absolutely, yes. So you have these people, placing the music – then you have to clear that music with the rights owners – typically you'll have two rights owners for every piece of recorded music: the people who own the songwriting element – the music publishers, which is what we do at Chrysalis – and the people who own the master recordings – which is usually the record company. You need to clear both rights. Typically you pay the same for each, but not always; sometimes you hit a hurdle because publishers want to clear at a certain rate, and the record companies want more. Or someone doesn't want to clear it at all! And just to make life even more confusing, where you have a record and a company that controls that recording, but songwriting – could be simple, one writer, could be six writers or ten writers – all with different publishers! It can get complicated.

There are probably many reasons – economic, artistic, cultural – why music and advertising, while closely connected, still have an uneasy relationship, and here Jeremy Lascelles identifies one of them in describing the difficulties of licensing. The tangle of writers, publishers and owners, all of whom need to be, paid illustrates how pressurised the humble song might be once at the centre of commercial interest. I wondered how the process might begin in the first place:

PM: To add another spin, how does a music supervisor get to choose that piece of music?

JL: Again, it's a multitude of different ways. What we do at Chrysalis music is that we regularly pitch music to all the people we know that are in those roles. We find out what they're looking for, while pitching the music generally, if we have a load of new stuff coming on – we get to know what they like and don't like, and their specific requirements. Sometimes they need, very specifically, a piece of 1950s BeBop jazz, sometimes it's much more of a mood thing . . . you sometimes get the description 'looking for a piece of music to do this . . .', which is such an extraordinarily broad, even lazy description, that it could be filled by anything from electronica to acoustic folk! So our brief is to regularly and creatively pitch music to these people, sometimes generally, sometimes specifically. They might come and say 'this is what we're looking for, for this particular ad or film' and we say 'well we think these pieces could work', and then the process goes on like that. Sometimes we pitch generally and it might take six months or a year for it to come to fruition; we might send a CD of a new act or a compilation with a theme to it, and it plants the seed in that person's mind and then later they'll come back to us because of it and it'll go ahead from there. It's not a straightforward process, really!

Working proactively in this way enables a company like Chrysalis Music to establish and maintain a key presence in the marketplace for advertising music; unlike independent labels, there is no one genre to which the company's catalogue is affiliated or associated, and so they can offer a full range of moods ('electronica to acoustic folk') and evocations of time and place ('a piece of 1950s BeBop jazz'). The key phrase here is 'creatively pitch music to these people'; that sense of proactivity is important, and shows the active pursuit of commissions and contracts – making things happen. Yet it seemed to me that the flow must sometimes run the other way:

PM: It must work the other way too; people come to you and say we need some music that does this thing or that thing . . .

JL: Sure, and if I may blow our own trumpet for a minute, when

I started working at Chrysalis in 1994 – a long time ago! – it was just at the start of recognisable pop tunes being used in a widespread way in commercials. There had been uses before of course, noticeable because of the novelty – the case of 'I Heard It Through the Grapevine' and 'Stand By Me' selling Levi jeans and so on – so I thought there's an opportunity here. At that time, record companies were completely passive in this area – if a request came along and the money was worthwhile they'd go 'OK great', but it was a very, very insignificant part of their overall business. Publishers were reactive rather than proactive for the most part, in fact; for example, EMI, then the biggest company by a long way, had one maybe two people who 'fielded' requests for music they published or owned. They didn't make any distinction between whether the request came for a movie, a TV show or a commercial. When I joined Chrysalis, I saw this opportunity and thought let's actually go and pitch music to the film, TV and ad makers – we're not getting many calls! So I appointed somebody to go out and do that, and divided the areas into different media types – so I built a department very quickly where I had one person who specialised in pitching music for commercials, one for film and one for TV, dealing with different people all the time. The film people and ad people are very different so I thought let's have specialists working with them. The results were instantaneous. We went from having very spasmodic use of our music in any of these fields to suddenly having things happen left right and centre!

So that department I think was the first dedicated to this kind of licensing, and remarkably so, for a company of our size. The model then became a kind of standard one, and as music use grew as a field of its own – people realised how financially lucrative it was – the publishing companies all started to build up their own areas, to be a little less reactive and put a bit more manpower into it. The trouble with a company as big as EMI Music is that they have so many songs that the phone does ring, all the time! So they make money without really having to do very much; a smaller company like Chrysalis, we can't afford to do that, so we have to go out and work to get things happening – and we do. We get results. From the perspective of the record companies, they used to consider this area as a just a little bit of extra that came along every now and again. Now, because of the steep decline in record sales, they're all looking for ways to make extra money as often as they can and they all have departments doing what we've been doing for years – looking to place their music in other media. So it's now become a fully staffed, sophisticated area of the industry, really, and of how you get your music exposed and not just that, a way to earn considerable revenue.

Lascelles had both the notion that this was an area worth moving into for his company and also the wit to develop a business model that would support it. He also introduces the idea of economies of scale – a company like EMI has a catalogue so large and wide that potential clients would be knocking on the door round the clock and can afford to be laissez-faire about the process. Chrysalis, while in no sense an independent label, has to work a little harder. This gave them a head start in this relatively new field, building in an active infrastructure, which has become increasingly significant while, as noted here, traditional income streams for the record companies have begun to dry up. So this kind of mediation of the music not only provides immediate income from the licensing fees, but offers potential promotional exposure for music both old and new. The Bob Dylan/ Co-op ad is one example of the former while Lascelles provides an excellent example of the latter:

PM: You mentioned the old Levi's ads – everyone already knew 'Stand By Me' [by Ben E. King] and the others and here was a new context to hear them in. Do you think it can work the other way round, that an ad can make a hit?

JL: Without any question, yes. It doesn't always, but it definitely can. Probably the best example I can give you from my experience is the Dandy Warhols, 'Bohemian Like You', which was used in a Vodafone ad in about 2000. The story behind that is quite a good one and illustrates how when it works it really can work. The Dandy Warhols had had a reasonably successful album, the previous album sold around 100,000 in the UK, a smallish hit but they were very much on the map. They then put out their follow-up album [*Thirteen Tales from Urban Bohemia*], and the first single was 'Bohemian Like You' and for one reason or another it completely tanked, which was extremely disappointing because I thought it was a really good record, but that's how these things work sometimes [the single came out first in September 2000 and got to number 42 in the UK chart]. So the single had stiffed, the album sold disappointingly, and it looked like 'game over' for the Dandy Warhols.

By good creative work on our team, we then managed, in the

summer of 2001, to get that song placed on the Vodafone ad, for reasonable money. Once it was on the ad, everyone said 'wow what's this great piece of music?' The record company woke up, said 'hey there's some attention being paid to the song again', re-released the single, it got to number 5 in November '01 – we're now talking fourteen months after its original release – and the album went on to be close to a platinum album. So it was a dead record, completely revitalised by its use in an ad and is now one of the most recognisable pieces around; you hear it all the time. I think the licensing of that one song, in Vodafone and other things, has brought in over a $100,000 in synchronisation income, purely for the licensing of the song, let alone any sales or PRS [Performing Rights Society] and so on. This is the most obvious example but there's lots of songs that have been broken by ads – the ad triggered interest in the song. The Jose Gonzales ['Heartbeats', used in an ad for the Sony Bravia LCD television], and plenty of others.

Equally it can work the other way – there was band called Stiltskin who had a Levi's ad; they were actually a 'manufactured' band, really – the guy behind them [songwriter Peter Lawlor] wrote jingles for a living and came out with this rock track and then decided to put a band together to front it up and perform it, to make it look 'real'. The single got to number one, a huge hit, but the band's credibility was nowhere, because people saw through it. In terms of it being a launch pad for a career, it was nowhere. You can say the same about – oh who were they? – Babylon Zoo, 'Spaceman'. Huge hit: career over! It sounds odd to say but success of the wrong sort can put an end to any prospect of a career. So the ad thing is a dangerous game, as those two acts discovered. That's the risk – short-term success – but is a short career better than no career at all? Maybe. The question is would they have had a career without the boost the ad gave them. Again, maybe.

This is a case study in itself of how a song may be 'made' by an advert in the case of the Dandy Warhols or, as Lascelles notes, it can work the other way as in the case of Babylon Zoo, where the success of 'Spaceman', used in a Levi's ad, effectively finished their career almost before it had begun. Clearly the formula does not always work. So what makes the difference? In some sense we are working once again with notions of the authentic; by 2000, the Dandy Warhols already had two albums and five years as signed recording artists to their

name; Babylon Zoo were, effectively, a new band launched in the marketplace via the Levi's ad. Looking at where the bands were written
about, we see quickly another difference in critical perception and
therefore mediation – the Dandy Warhols were, in the summer of
2000, interviewed in *Q*, *Mojo*, *Uncut* and the *NME*, as well as splashes
in the arts pages of the British broadsheets. Babylon Zoo, in contrast,
were interviewed and granted front pages in *Smash Hits*, *Sugar* and
Top of the Pops 'teen' magazines in the summer of 1996. The band also
drew the interest of daily tabloid newspapers – as did, it should be said,
Oasis at this time, often in the same issue. This is telling too in that
the success of 'Spaceman' coincided with the height of the first wave
of the so-called 'Britpop' movement and their retro-futuristic musical
and visual stylings were notably out of step with the wider mood of
the time; outside the bubble of the advert they seemed isolated. Yet by
2000 the Dandy Warhols found their similarly retro stylings borrowed
from established models of rock authenticity to be wholly harmonious
with contemporary tastes. The ebb and flow of taste can also therefore have a strong influence on what succeeds and what does not and
furthermore cannot be anticipated with absolute confidence.

Issues of liveness are brought into consideration too. The Dandy
Warhols were an established live act with a strong reputation for an
excellent show and routinely selling out college-sized venues. Babylon
Zoo, in contrast, never gave a live performance. Likewise, the nature
of marketing and media presence of each band outside the context of
the advertising has an effect on subsequent success. The DWs were,
despite some initial bridling, accepted by the UK music press as a band
worthy of attention; yet we note that both bands were signed to EMI
labels. 'Bohemian Like You' has gained multiple uses in film (e.g. *Igby
Goes Down*, 2002), TV (e.g. *Match of the Day*, BBC) and advertising
(e.g. the 'Next' clothing chain) since this breakthrough exposure and
the band built a very successful career upon the back of this acclaim.
Here, the formula succeeded, with the fortunate alignment of a substantial group of cultural variables. With Babylon Zoo, such variables
could be seen to have conspired against sustained success – as far as
Levi's and the agency were concerned, the 'Spaceman' ad would be
judged a success. It did its job, garnering great publicity and a renewed
commercial presence for the brand. For EMI and Babylon Zoo, the
question is more difficult to answer – we note that the Dandy Warhols
are still working and recording, while Babylon Zoo were dropped by
EMI after their second album, and a career considered by cultural
gatekeepers as 'a fluke in the first place' (*NME* review of Babylon
Zoo album *King Kong Groover* (EMI) 2 January 1999). This is the

great weight of backstory and problematic variables behind Jeremy Lascelles' 'Maybe'.

Moving on from this case study, we discussed the importance or otherwise of artist approval in the licensing of music to advertising.

> PM: Given the potential for success or failure, what role is given to artist approval?
>
> JL: That's a key question, it's very important. Because in our contracts we give all our writers and all our artists the right of approval for any use of their music; it just seems right and proper. To give a crass example, if the singer is a vegetarian and we wanted a song to advertise McDonald's . . . so we give them right to refrain from approval, even in some of the really old contracts where that right isn't expressed directly we still go to them and say are you cool with this. You don't want to do something disrespectful or offensive to the creator of that work. So there are lots of artists – although fewer than there were – who are adamant, militant even about what happens to their songs. Some have a real hard line – fine on a case-by-case basis in the right kind of film or TV, but never in commercials. That's changing, however, simply because more and more music is being used in commercials so it sticks out less –so people who would never have let their music be used in commercials before, like Bob Dylan, now let it happen. So I use that sometimes with our writers – if Dylan can say yes, you ought to say yes! I'm thinking of that ad with John Lennon – no music but he's talking as if on a chat show about how change is good, how it has to happen and so on . . . it's a car ad or an insurance ad and I went 'woh!' and I know a lot of people are uncomfortable about it . . . it feels wrong, but Yoko Ono has clearly approved it.

This issue of artist approval, as Klein noted, has led to a number of disputed and controversial cases. Here we are dealing with issues of cultural and, sometimes, subcultural capital as both Muggleton (2000; Muggleton and Weinzerl 2003) and Thornton (1995) have speculated. Taking the case of Nick Drake's 'Pink Moon' as our starting point, I asked Jeremy Lascelles what he thought was at stake here.

> PM: So if there is artist approval, why do you think there is sometimes resistance from fans to music being used in this way? I'm thinking particularly of the use of Nick Drake's 'Pink Moon' by Volkswagen which sent the hardcore fans apoplectic.

JL: The use of 'Pink Moon' in that ad was a real breakthrough. Drake was still a very underground, cult artist at that point, and that ad was the catalyst that exposed his music to a huge audience. I would argue that without it considerably fewer people in the world would know his music than currently do. As you know his music was known by very few during his lifetime, which is a very sad state of affairs, but now, partly thanks to the ad, they do. My view is this: if you're making a decision about a piece of music by an established artist there are two things to consider – one is obviously the money, are they paying well enough, and the other is the product – is it one you'd feel OK or terrible about endorsing, and is the quality of the visuals all it should be? If it passes all or maybe even two out of the three you'd probably do it. Damon Albarn, for example, whom we publish – not the Blur stuff but we publish his current things – will let his music be used for commercials, but only if he feels the product is something worthwhile; so the British Gas commercial is OK [an instrumental excerpt from Blur's 'The Universal'], but not one for, say Hummer cars or something like that. That seems to be an acceptable way to use the control you have over how your music is placed.

PM: Value and meaning aggregates around certain songs and artists, and there arises this secret brotherhood of admirers to whom it is more than a matter of commerce – there's something proprietorial about it.

JL: Well that was certainly the case with the Nick Drake example, but I think you get that with lots of artists. If you have someone who is your private passion and then all of a sudden they break through, and it doesn't have to be via a commercial, wide commercial success can really upset you. It's out there in the wider world; my hunch is that the fans who were upset by that [the 'Pink Moon' episode] would have been upset had he become more widely known via any other means . . . become a popular artist rather than a hidden secret.

There is a trade-off here – acknowledging the interest that music has for advertisers and also being mindful that at least part of what an advertiser is hoping will rub off onto the product as borrowed interest is precisely that perceived cultural value which is most at risk from the song being used to sell something. When tunes from that most connoisseurial repertoire – Northern Soul – were used to sell Kentucky Fried Chicken in the early 2000s as 'Soul Food' there was a great wave of dissent from the Northern Soul subcultural constituency, causing a resentment which still persists. Lascelles spoke about why he thinks these kind of reactions among a fanbase are not unusual, and more widely about the perceived value, commercial and aesthetic, of popular music recordings as marketplace entities.

JL: You're always going to get that response I suppose but because it's now so widespread [music in ads] there's less reason to be offended, in the main, unless something is done in a particularly crass way. I don't like it when songs are rewritten for ads.

PM: Such as the 2009 Muller yogurt ad that rewrites Nina Simone's 'I Got Life'?

JL: Exactly, but the final argument is that it's the responsibility of the guardians of the songs, that is the publishers and writers and record companies, to use their discretion. We live in a commercial world and money talks. Sometimes record companies will say 'I want this song on this ad, because it's great exposure, and by the way I want you to give it away for free', and I say 'No, we shouldn't give it away for free . . . it may be great exposure, but the artist has a right to be paid. So if you give records away for free – which actually we do, sometimes! [laughs] – it leads in to one of the biggest problems facing the record industry. That is that it has effectively devalued its product by giving it away too often; so you have the notion that music is a cheap or valueless commodity, when it is one of the most precious things you can own! Some of the records I bought when I was a kid are still among my most treasured possessions, those records changed my life, and they probably cost me 30 shillings at the time. Let's update that – if I buy a great CD for £10 or £12 today – and most cost a lot less than that – and I carry on enjoying it for thirty years, what else at that level gives you that much pleasure back? Yet the public think that £10 or £12 is way too much for a CD! That's the record companies managing to mess things up, as they have done historically, by giving things away. But we're getting off the subject here!

PM: No, not at all, because it's to do with the idea of the value of music isn't it, and that's why they want music in their ads because they hope some of the beauty or charm or reputation or perceived value, cultural or economic, will somehow 'rub off' on the car or sofa or whatever it is that they want us to buy.

JL: That's absolutely right, they want the music to provide a gloss which surrounds the product, whether that's a movie or a can of Coke, trainers or a car.

The root of the relationship between music and advertising is the specially commissioned tune or 'jingle'. Coca-Cola has a very long history of the advertising jingle, from very early tunes to specially written tunes by the likes of Jack White of the White Stripes (see *The Independent*, 29 April 2006: 'Jack White "sells out" by recording song for Coca-Cola advertisement'). The more contemporary tunes rarely mention the product but let the link between pictures and sounds establish the commercial bridges more organically – contrast, for example, Ray Charles' handful of Coke commercials in the 1950s and 1960s (e.g. 'Coke has a taste you'll never get tired of . . .') with Jack White's opaquely referential tune ('What Goes Around Comes Around') from 2006. Despite the fact that artists as influential and enduring as Charles, Aretha Franklin and Marvin Gaye had all recorded several Coke jingles between them, a section of White's fan base was appalled at his decision to collaborate with Coca-Cola in this way, a throwback to the era where 'real' rock music was very rarely associated with commercial products – indeed, this may well have been partly why White decided to take the commission. Perhaps he just like the red and white colour scheme of Coke's livery, as all White Stripes product was decked in red and white. Perhaps it was the substantial fee. Regardless of his motivation, it was an unusual move which combined elements of the specially composed jingle with the kudos of having a real rock star associated with the product. In this it is possibly the ideal dynamic for a product like Coca-Cola.

I wondered how Jeremy Lascelles felt that the music industry viewed these kinds of dynamics within the buying and selling of music as part of advertising:

PM: Has the dominance of the 'bought in' song effectively put an end to the tradition of the advertising 'jingle' or do you still deal with this kind of music?

JL: A little bit, yes – and funnily enough, when you hire someone to write specifically for a jingle, it's much cheaper than just licensing an existing piece of music. It's ironic but creation is cheaper than hiring! Those things tend to operate – not always but tend to – operate on the buy-out. So the composer is paid a fee, a fixed fee for a specific job; it's true to say that you tend to get fairly poorly paid. We have done those with some of our writers but the more lucrative, financially and by far, is the licensing. It's not always well known things, though and I'll give you an example. Do you remember one of the great ads of the last ten years or so, the Guinness ad – the horses? The soundtrack for that is Leftfield, one of our groups. The story behind that is the visuals existed for that well in advance and they either had a piece of music in there that they couldn't clear, they couldn't afford or just weren't happy with. The girl who then ran our film and TV department was contacted by the ad agency because they knew that we were very good at supplying things; they sent her the visuals and we'd just received the new Leftfield album – they'd had a huge album previously [*Leftism*, Chrysalis 1995] and we got this advance copy, it wasn't coming out for a few months, and Tracy started playing around with a few things and came up with this bit of the track ['Phat Planet'] that had some rolling drumbeats, they thought it worked, and they fell in love with it. We thought it was great too, it got a reasonable amount of money and great advance publicity; the band were interested but the record company initially didn't want it to happen because they thought 'we can't let this music out three months in advance of the release of the album'; it wasn't the single they were planning and so on. But they did relent. So the ad came out and no one knew what it was at first, and then the word on the grapevine started to get out, that it was Leftfield, and that became a very important part of that album when it came out a couple of months later [*Rhythm and Stealth*, Chrysalis 1999]. So it wasn't a familiar piece of music at the time, and everyone remembers the ad; it was extremely distinctive in the way it was used.

PM: That's great because people want to know what it is . . .

JL: It was a double win, great publicity and it made money! So when people say 'you have to put this song out for free, it'll be great publicity, I think of the Leftfield story! I do think it is the right of the owner and creator of a piece of music to get paid. How else do they earn a living?

Leftfield's commercial success was hugely increased by the use of their music in the Guinness 'Sea Horses' ad and, equally importantly perhaps, did not diminish their critical standing. This is partly due to the product – a popular, expensive, stylish drink – and partly due to the social context, as all things Irish were very marketable in the late 1990s as the Celtic Tiger economy gathered pace and heat. Finally it was also due to the innovative nature of the visuals – the sound and the pictures made for a very powerful match. The happy accident which led to this connection cannot be planned or replicated – it just 'happened'. In an increasingly risk-averse music industry these coincidences may happen less frequently than they did, but this example illuminates what can happen when the balance is right. Leftfield's success, like that of the Dandy Warhols, shows how Chrysalis Music has succeeded in this complex marketplace; the pair of songs are among the most popular and effective examples of music in advertising over the past decade, and in both cases the artists benefited substantially from the exposure.

What the use of music in advertising and indeed in the wider fields of film and TV delivers is not merely a little more recognition in the listener or viewer but a third entity which draws on the two independent elements yet stands free of them. I wondered if any particular genre has proved more popular or better suited to this complex task.

PM: Do certain areas of your catalogue prove more popular for ads and licensed use than others?

JL: It's very cyclical. There was a period of time, in the lateish 90s and early 2000s, where electronic music like Leftfield and Aphex Twin, whom we publish, was extremely popular. The Chemical Brothers, instrumental electronic music, very rhythmically based; Propellerheads was another one ['History Repeating' featuring Shirley Bassey, 1997], everyone wanted that, that was the soundbed of so many ads around that time. So we did extremely well in that genre; that sort of thing then ran its course, as things do in pop and commerce, and the trend moved towards other things – two or three years ago there was a big trend toward acoustic, new folk kind of sound, so you'd get Vashti Bunyan used, Jose Gonzales, that acoustic-folky, very dreamy sound. You can't predict and it also goes round and round in circles! With Leftfield we did fantastically well, licensed in all sorts of ways and uses, and then it slowed down and we haven't had call for the likes of Leftfield and the electronic stuff in the last few years but it will come round again.

As he notes here, things run their course 'in pop and commerce' and what proves a great double win in one musical or commercial era might not succeed in another – consider how 'dated' (or 'retro', according to preference) the music and ads of the 1970s or 1980s seem in contrast to contemporary equivalents. Yet all have had their moment and run their course. The wheel turns. As it does so, it can throw up the unexpected, and often it is the relatively unheard or unknown music which functions most effectively – Jeremy Lascelles refers here to Vashti Bunyan's song 'Another Diamond Day', which received exposure by being used in a T-Mobile advert in 2006. It has several links with the Nick Drake example; like 'Pink Moon' it was the title track of an album produced by Joe Boyd and which Bunyan issued in 1970. Like *Pink Moon* it sank without trace commercially at the time but in the intervening decades, through a slow process of word of mouth and its great rarity, became prized as a cult object – a perfect example of cultural capital being transferred to an obscure artefact. Unlike the Drake catalogue the album was unavailable for nearly thirty years and when the album was reissued in 2000 it was, as often happens, 'rediscovered' by the new heritage industry of monthly rock magazines and radio, all hungry for something fresh to explore and explain. The story was perfect – Bunyan had quit the music industry after the album's failure and could, in every sense, be 'rediscovered'; unlike Nick Drake, she could take up where she left off and her career resumed and she recorded a second album with a number of her new and younger admirers. The use of her music – pastoral, lilting, somewhat fey but undeniably charming – was a new flavour in advertising, seeking to link mobile phone technologies to broader notions of an ergonomic, organic 'lifestyle'.

This was in contrast to established models, such as in the contemporary success of the Dandy Warhols tune for rival mobile company Vodafone, where exciting, big beat music suggested life lived in fast, bright and ceaseless movement. The use of Bunyan's song, accompanied by slow-motion images showing the physical realities of the street being bent gently out of shape just enough to be interesting, strove for a sense of contemplation, even meditation. It proved very successful for T-Mobile and for Bunyan, who experienced a surge in sales of her thirty-year old album similar to those experienced by Drake's *Pink Moon*. A similar technique was applied to the mix of Jose Gonzales' cover of the Knife's 'Heartbeats' and the memorable slow-motion 'coloured balls' ad, tumbling down the hills of San Francisco, put together for Sony Bravia televisions. This style, as Jeremy Lascelles says, did well in this marketplace for a while and then, like the taste for electronic which preceded it, it was itself superseded and forms which reflected desired versions of contemporary realities found its place.

If pop means 'a million and one things' then we need to be cautious about ascribing generic terminology to its mediation – as far as advertising's approach to pop goes, using the Archies' 'Sugar Sugar' to advertise breakfast cereal for children is drawing from the same well as, say, using Gang of Four's 'Natural's Not In It' to advertise the XBox Kinect as it has been in 2010–11. Within the local ideology of rock and pop, of course, there is a world of difference, yet advertising functions as a kind of leveller. The original marxist-intellectual ideological drive of the Gang of Four's work on albums such as 1979's *Entertainment!* is arguably compromised by licensing their music to an advert but, one might note, they were always fully aware that putting music out into the marketplace, price tag attached, was in itself a contradiction (see Mills 1994; Hoover 1998; Lester 2008). Consequently they acknowledge that all music is for sale, and that if it is to be heard, understood, enjoyed, then this is the hidden cost to the artist – art becomes commodity. Furthermore pop is well-suited to the job asked of it by advertising in that its information and impact comes in concise, punchy packages (certainly compared to the wider spaces in which jazz and classical repertoires thrive) and can convey a lot of excitement and energy quickly and directly, 'especially in an advert where you only have a minute or so to do the job'. The 'accidental' success of Leftfield could not be predicted; another Chrysalis act, the Proclaimers, experienced something similar when their song 'I'm Gonna Be (500 Miles)' was used in the movie *Benny and Joon* in 1993. As Proclaimer Charlie Reid's sleeve note on their *Best Of* album explains, the song's presence in the film was pure serendipity:

> Mary Stuart Masterson was playing the song a lot on the set of *Benny and Joon* and it became a favourite with the crew and was included on the soundtrack . . . We wrote her a note . . . we owe her a very large drink.

That 'very large drink' is owed by many musicians to the use adverts, TV and film have made of their music; yet it is a field in which success cannot be guaranteed, may rebound badly on the music, product or artist (such as the disastrous series of Pepsi ads in the late 1980s with Michael Jackson and Madonna), or it may change the lives and careers of those involved (Dandy Warhols, Leftfield, Vashti Bunyan). As Jeremy Lascelles says in conclusion, music and the impact that it has does not work to or conform to a formula, as an advertiser or film-maker paying well for its use might wish that it did. Its impact cannot be guaranteed, regardless of what we might read. Music exists and is free; that is precisely what the licensee is paying for, but there is no certainty that they will get the return they are looking for. Images can be manipulated but music cannot; it is beyond absolute and final editorial control and must find its own course.

Advertising exercises

1. What 'borrowed interest' do advertisers seek when they license a song? What risks are there for the artist?

2. Taking Coca-Cola as an example, research the history of the 'jingle'. Is the 'jingle' dead?

3. Find out about Volkswagen's use of Nick Drake's song 'Pink Moon'. Do you think that his family should have allowed the use? If not, why not?

4. Why might fans object to their favourite music being used in adverts?

4 Who Listens to the Radio? Popular Music and Public Service Radio

To discuss radio services is to stumble immediately into the art versus commerce debate – characterised here by public service versus commercial radio broadcasting. As James Addyman mentions here, this is an area of dispute which is as old as the medium itself yet one which is renewed each time the technologies which deliver the words and music change and develop. As with other media, such as video, computing and the talking picture, music has played a central role in the development of radio as a genuinely popular and democratic medium – that is often what listeners turn to the radio in search of – and the spread of musical styles beyond their immediate localities. Unlike television or in the cinema radio makes the experience of listening to and enjoying music portable; listening in the car or moving round the house or workplace with a battery-powered set frees the listener from the fixed seat required by the visual spectacle. This changes the listener's relationship with the music in that one may choose to take it with you or leave it where it is – and one may also tune away, return later or change genre at a moment's notice. So radio tends to drift toward being genre-specific in its musical vocabulary, and the BBC's radio structure since the creation of Radios 1, 2, 3 and 4 in 1967 has been precisely thus. These channels were a rearrangement of the BBC's radio output after the Marine Offences Act of 1967 wiped out the unlicensed offshore commercial or 'pirate' radio stations such as Radio Caroline which played popular music to large audiences (see Conway 2009 and Johns 2010, for example). Formerly there had been the Home Service offering news, talk and discussion, the Light Programme which delivered entertainment and 'light' or popular music, and the Third Programme, which took a major role in developing the place of the arts in British society.

In their stead came Radio 1, taking the place of the pirate stations in offering current pop music, Radio 2 which offered light and middle of the road music, Radio 3 the classical music repertoire and Radio 4 bringing news and current affairs, informed discussion and comment, drama and comedy. It's remarkable to note that it was 1967 – the so-called Summer of Love, at least four years after the arrival of Beatlemania and all that that implies – before the UK had a national popular music radio station. It is worth noting too that while Radio 4 has been the subject of sustained study (see Hendy 200; Elmes 2008), as has Radio 3 (Carpenter 1996), the history of Radio 1 has yet to be properly recorded – the most substantial work on the station (Garfield 1999) was an oral history focusing on a specific period and Osborne (2009) only lightly touches upon the role of BBC radio in the mediation of pop. This early institutional inertia toward the new music was not entirely shaken off after 1967 and the early 1970s saw the BBC seeking to reduce its music broadcasting via the 'needletime' dispute (needletime being the amount of a show occupied by playing recorded music and which the BBC had to pay for) and brought Radios 1 and 2 together in the mornings and afternoons to cut costs, to the dismay of some of its listeners.

Yet the service was extremely popular. In cahoots with BBC 1's *Top of the Pops*, the DJs became stars and Radio 1 at first easily saw off the first new regional stations granted licences from 1973 onwards. Yet this change allowed independent local radio such as Piccadilly in Manchester and Radio City in Liverpool to test the BBC's provision in those areas – thus the centralised programming of the BBC was required to work more efficiently within its budget in order to fulfil the corporation's remit and make a case for staying on air. So distinctive programming became more important than ever, yet has historically been undervalued by the BBC. For example, John Peel (see Peel 2006) put his remarkable ability to survive the management comings and goings at Radio 1 down to him being the station's 'pet rebel', retained not for itself but because his show's presence on the schedules was tangible evidence that the station was meeting its public service obligation. Thus we have a paradox – music programming is one of the most direct ways to conceive of, make real and deliver the somewhat chimeric notion of 'distinctive programming' yet it is often one of the most conservative areas of BBC policy.

In order to address this puzzle, we now consider two examples of specialist music programming, the type of broadcasting which is both under threat from yet unique to public service radio. One is nationally broadcast, BBC Radio 3's *Late Junction*, the other springs from the BBC's regional output, *Down in the Grooves*, made and broadcast by BBC Radio Leeds. Both seem to embody and protect something of what Canadian band Rush called 'The Spirit of Radio'.

The national specialist show, *Late Junction*, BBC Radio 3

Fiona Talkington is the original presenter of the BBC Radio 3 show *Late Junction* which remains a unique presence in national radio broadcasting in the UK, and is particularly renowned for the bold eclecticism of its content which frequently seems to 'break the rules' set by most genre-specific radio broadcasting. Talkington presented the very first edition of the show on 13 September 1999 and, with her colleague Verity Sharp, still carries the soul of the show with her. This passion for the music is frequently recognised by listeners and by their industry peers – for example, the show won a 'Sony' Gold award in 2003 for Music Programming, and the citation included the following summary:

> *Late Junction* is a radio jewel. Is there a show like this anywhere else in the radio world? Everyone who hears the show falls in love with it. Surprising, revealing, accessible. Brilliantly programmed – a show where the real star is the music.

On the show's tenth birthday in November 2009 a special concert was held at the new Kings Place Arts Centre at King's Cross in London and Roger Wright, Controller of Radio 3 and Director of the Proms, observed that

> *Late Junction* has gone from strength to strength and its eclectic programming has won awards, critical acclaim and a loyal listenership. Radio 3's *Late Junction* offers a way into worlds of music which might not otherwise be heard at all.

Talkington's own tireless enthusiasm for Norwegian music was formally recognised when in 2004 she was awarded the Molde Rose at the Molde International Jazz Festival, only the second time that this prize (commemorating contributions to Norwegian culture) has been awarded to a non-Norwegian. Further to this, in 2009 she was awarded the Royal Norwegian Order of Merit for her championing of Norwegian arts. Clearly the show is felt to have made a substantial contribution not only to the dissemination of less well-known musics but to their being part of a wider musical vocabulary, pointing up connections between apparently unrelated musical forms. This is both a challenge for and a virtue of the mediation of music via radio.

The programme covers a wide range of styles and musical vocabularies, not for the sake of it, but in pursuit of connections and perhaps unexpected meeting points of tradition and innovations– hence the title of the show. As Fiona Talkington mentions in the piece below, the show grows out of what Radio 3 already does rather than being at odds with the parent station. As the original presenter, she has been central to the programme since its very inception, and I asked her how she came to be working for BBC Radio 3.

PM: What was your background in radio and how did you arrive at Radio 3?

FT: Before Radio 3 I worked for independent local radio in Reading, in the days when ILR had lots of varied and interesting musical programming, before they went for the computer playlist approach. So I used to present a classical programme on there once a week, and after a couple of years they decided they were going to axe all the specialist programmes, and someone said to me 'why don't you send a demo tape to Radio 3', which I did. This was 1989. So I started presenting as part of a team on a programme called 'Mainly For Pleasure' which was the 'drivetime' show before the current 'In Tune'. I got to choose the music when I was presenting and then a couple of years later they axed that programme too! After that I became a general announcer for Radio 3 which was actually just fantastic, because it's such a broad station that I could be reading the news, or presenting the Proms, or a Wigmore Hall concert, Composer of the Week, the afternoons . . . I ended up presenting right across the whole spectrum of programmes. There were lots of opportunities for live broadcasting, for making features and for sneaking in bits of music that I thought weren't getting an airing anywhere else – and that's probably where things began to change for me a little.

Talkington's initial experience is illustrative of the changes that came upon 'ILR' (independent local radio – that is local radio not run by the BBC) with the centralisation of playlists and the switch from analogue sources (tape and disc) to digital – initially compact disc and then eventually, as she mentions, 'the computer playlist approach'. In 1997, RAJAR figures showed that ILR had 51.7 per cent of potential listeners and looked as if they would supersede the then very shaky BBC. However, this surge of popularity proved its undoing, as it became clear there was money to be made from buying the stations and acquiring the licences to broadcast; the launch of Virgin Radio in 1992 is an example of this process just as it was getting into gear, a process which would end in farce once it had been bought by Chris Evans, a road which led to mutual ruin. As Stoller (2010) notes, 'independent radio became commercial radio' – that is advertising rather than content driven – so output became blander and less distinctive, as we see here in Fiona Talkington's experience: 'they decided they were going to axe all the specialist programmes'. Her idea of 'sneaking in bits of music that weren't getting an airing anywhere else' is a little hint at the roots of *Late Junction* itself, and also the pleasure to be taken from finding a place for the lesser known musical voice within mainstream programming. I pressed her on this aspect of her approach to presenting music on the radio.

PM: What kind of 'bits' do you mean? Obscure areas of the classical repertoire ?

FT: Not really – although that was quite handy too – it was more, for example, take one of Greig's lyric pieces, 'Arietta', a beautiful piano piece but Jan Gabarek also plays it on the saxophone, so why shouldn't Radio 3 be playing that? Or music by Bartók – why shouldn't we play it performed by all sorts of different musicians. Why can't you play his piano music next to recordings of the traditional songs, where those tunes come from? It just made sense to me. I was once presenting a morning programme called 'Musical Encounters' in the early 90s and I could choose an 'Artist of the Week', so I chose Jan Garbarek. The producers were quite shocked and said 'Oh we couldn't possibly have that'. But I won, and I interviewed him, which was the first time there had been an artist interview on that show. I thought all that was a real achievement, as it was doing something different, playing excellent quality music by an outstanding musician who had every right to be on Radio 3, and not just in the ghetto hours of jazz programming or whenever it might be. The point was to make people listen to music in a different way, to put things side by side and show the connections. So I just tried to do that whenever I had the opportunity.

PM: This sounds like the roots of *Late Junction* – did somebody hear and pick up on that and say 'that's a good idea', and then develop something on those lines? How did your connection with the show initially come about?

FT: Well, during those early years on Radio 3 Nicolas Kenyon was Controller, and was also Director of the Proms, and when he went off to do that full time Roger Wright took over. One day he said to me 'Fiona, if I was thinking of starting a programme where you might play Jan Gabarek alongside Bulgarian Chant and ECM New Series what would you think?' I said, 'you know exactly what I'd think, which I guess is why you're asking me.'

And a programme was born! We started talking about it with producers, Verity Sharp came on board as the other presenter and we decided two weeks on and two weeks off, sharing the presentation, would probably work well in terms of workload and continuity. Verity Sharp was working in Birmingham for Radio 3 on a young person's programme called 'Making Tracks', and she was into all sorts of music.

Here we see how a distinctive piece of media programming might be years in the making yet seem to fall together and 'happen' almost without design – 'a programme was born!' – but, as she notes, not without a fight. As she observes regarding the discussion concerning the Norwegian saxophonist Jan Garbarek, she 'won' that round and made sure that this kind of content was more likely to be suggested and to be accepted as part of what the station played. It might be simply a shuffling of the pack at the top end of a particular media institution which can make a difference – one controller is succeeded by another with slightly different interests – or it might be a change in the marketplace, from vinyl to CD, or new sources coming to the fore such as the influx of Eastern European music in the late 1980s and early 1990s, and the distributive infrastructures of the music industry developing as a global phenomenon alongside the rise of the download. Suddenly, not only was there all this material available, there was a potential demand for it. I wondered how the show was allowed to develop once it had been begun.

PM:　When it began, was there any prescription or direction in terms of the musical policy of the show or was it just left to you?

FT:　There was no policy; no one said you've got to have this amount of world music, or jazz, or classical. We thought about musical areas – it being late at night then obviously something like Arvo Pärt from contemporary classical is perfect, and then exploring the music of other continents. In truth, if you're doing a programme properly, you should be able to make it from what you have at home, simply bringing in stuff. If someone asks you to do a programme, you can usually do it from what you've got at home – it's like having someone round to dinner, 'oh now listen to this, what do you think?' We all had things that we were desperate to share with other people. So it was more to do with putting together a musical sequence that we liked and were passionate about and by looking at that you begin to see patterns that were emerging.

You could have some African kora music next to Gregorian chant and for me it especially meant there was a place for the Nordic music that I was really into. It also provided the chance to explore down where the dust had collected in the BBC gramophone library, all the field recordings and so on – just to be able to try things. We were going out four nights a week initially, so we could take risks and try things. It's not about playing music that people are going to love, but about music that people are going to experience – if you go into a gallery you don't want to buy every painting you see but you want to know they're there and experience them.

I did the very first show and I began with a Swedish vocal trio, singing a little fisherman's prayer – I thought 'Radio 3, we do trios, we do choral music, let's have this'. So it grew out of Radio 3, what we were already doing, it wasn't 'you're not playing this so I'm going to make you play it'. The mixture of reflection and letting people know what's out there – not big presentation, not big interviews or a magazine programme, but just 'here's some music'.

PM: This was music that you'd have difficulty hearing anywhere else, even today.

FT: Yes that was the feedback we got in the early days, that either people hadn't heard music like this, and didn't even know it existed in some cases, or just saying thank you, we can't get this music anywhere else at all. So we knew we were doing something right as the feedback was so good.

So the show was born out of the interest, expertise and opportunity to share granted to a group of media professionals – yet this does not guarantee that a show will find an audience. In fact it could be argued that there is a reason why supposed 'minority musics' are precisely that – there is little proven marketplace demand for them. Bearing this in mind, I wondered how the show sets about drawing in and keeping an audience via the key component – the music. Further, if music radio is almost exclusively genre driven, what is the logic of a show which breaks all these programming rules?

PM: The show also seems interested in drawing an audience by making, or illuminating, connections between apparently unrelated musical vocabularies – would you say this is fair comment?

FT: Definitely. It is about connections. Sometimes it can be a very obvious one – say, a kora and a lute, which leads onto a banjo, more playful then onto a dobro and so on . . . you can play that game, or when you listen to things there might be a little falling phrase that you've heard in a piano piece by Liszt that just happens to be the main motif in a melody sung by a Polynesian choir. These musical coincidences across the globe have become a very *Late Junction* signature element, and why shouldn't we put them together? We don't mean one is necessarily inspired by the other – how could they be – but it's just trying to make people listen, to open up their ears. Just this morning I was planning a programme and I had this track by Cesario Evora and wondering what to play next I just thought 'Duke Ellington'. Now why I thought of him is a moot point but it's something about the mood, the feel, where I wanted to go next, using that instinct. Before the first programme the powers that be said 'Are we going to be able to see some playlists before the show?' I replied 'well if you saw the playlists you wouldn't know what was the title of the song and which was the name of the artist', so the playlist stayed between the producer and myself.

This illustrates a key point about the role of the 'powers that be' in controlling a programme's output, and the issue of keeping a station's output recognisable if not quite homogenous – the playlist would have left the reader no wiser, so it 'stayed between the producer and myself'. In some ways this is a throwback to an era when programme makers drove their own shows and selected their own content, free of internal or external influence. As far as the BBC goes, even the specialist programming (evenings and weekends slots) on Radios 1 and 2 is heavily guided by playlists, record company release schedules and unwritten agreements between wings of the industry. *Late Junction*, while exposed to some of these pressures, seems to have retained much of that original sense of being driven by internal, musical logic rather than business and/or institutional logic. In this the programme resembles the programmes of John Peel and Charlie Gillett in the 1970s.

> PM: Adorno wrote about 'active' and passive' listening and there's some of that here, isn't there – actually focusing on the music – but there's also the idea that ideas come between the listener and the music, that theory of 'not listening' because of the ideological clutter . . . 'I can't like that because I don't like that style or I've never listened to that instrument before'. It comes between you and the music. *Late Junction* doesn't suffer from that, and often

the listener won't even know what they're singing about! So you listen differently.

FT: Yes, but it's also about the obsession with instant gratification, culturally, and that doesn't impact on us – it's fine for us to play 'challenging' things – in fact people might hate some of the things we play – I remember when we played Gavin Bryers we received huge numbers of complaints 'what's this dreadful music, take it off!', or when we played a piece by Charlemagne Palestine which was just one chord for 40 minutes, people said 'switch it off!' but I'm not going to! You can engage with this in a different way, or not, but you have to give people the opportunity – it's not just a three and a half minute track, it's about reacting and moving on, learning without being taught.

Here is a challenge to the notion that music radio should merely serve the existing interests of the audience or the marketing and release schedules of the powerful record company. So there is a zealous quality to the programming ('but I'm not going to!') which is also an educative one ('learning without being taught'). The latter is especially important, as effectively *Late Junction* invites and allows its audience to listen to the music unencumbered and leaves it free to respond. So I wondered whether this was driven by the presenters or the producers?

PM: Do you choose the music? Or is it driven by the producer or a powerful record company that has what it thinks are new releases which would be perfectly promoted by a slot on *Late Junction*?

FT: It's definitely not the record company. Ultimately it's down to the presenter. We do our own playlists. We work with just one producer for any given fortnight and they are supposed to come up with a pile of discs they think are interesting and with them you might explore a theme, such as, say, lullabies or wedding rituals and the producer will do the hard graft gathering examples from around the world through the music library at the BBC. But really the playlists come out of my house!

PM: And was it like that from the first show?

FT: Yes, pretty much, we worked for a presenter called Anthony Pitts in the early days, who was very involved with the show, the main producer at the start. He was a composer and he took a great interest in the playlists and would want to work with us on them. He had a really wide repertoire of musical knowledge and it was great to work with him in those early days because he could find unusual things when we really wanted them, contrasting but related material. So producers have come and gone and we've worked with them but right at the heart of it is the same desire – we pick up a CD and say I love this and want people to hear it. What has changed, in some ways, is that in the beginning people loved us for everything we played because they didn't know this music and now people do know more about music and know more about the wider musical world so they can be a bit more critical – 'oh, you played that piece by Keith Jarrett but actually the recording by this Brazilian player is better'! So people's knowledge has really grown. I think *Late Junction* has contributed to this growth and the audience seems to agree.

PM: Because they've learned without being taught.

The division of labour between presenter and producer is instructive and ensures that the programme retains a mixed input as producers have 'come and gone'. So there are consistent elements to the content, and this has in time created a change in the audience's response to that content. As Fiona Talkington says, the programme has discreetly educated its audience and, very properly, the attentive listener is now well placed to be more critical and assume the mantle of the connoisseur or, indeed, a gatekeeper of sorts. So while the influence of the show has clearly grown, I wondered where she saw the show sitting with the UK World Music industry, as explored in the section on independent labels and the case study of *Songlines* magazine.

PM: How do you feel *Late Junction* fits into the World Music 'industry', that circuit of the magazines, the festivals, the independent labels and so on?

FT: It's definitely got a foot in there . . . but one thing that really irritates me is the fact that *Late Junction* is on the 'World Music' pages of the Radio 3 website, because we do play 'world music', but we also play classical, blues, folk, electronica and spoken word and non-classifiable and I could go on! The show has had bad press over this – people say 'oh that dreadful world music programme *Late Junction*' and I think 'Well I played some really beautiful Schubert last night' or some contemporary classical music, so I think having that World Music label on us hasn't helped. So I think we have a foot in that World Music industry but I do draw back a little bit at this impression of it being the kind of Starbucks version of it where everything's smiley and smells of coffee beans, and we know that that's not true! Also I think World Music awards have been, I think, quite label and promoter driven where a true 'world music' award would be finding the little old man in the valley in southern Italy singing Tarantella songs in the same way for sixty years. We also want to embrace new artists of real quality, who've got their roots in a tradition and are able to move that tradition on, without losing the soul of it. The bad news is when someone who just wants to be a diva in the West and will only sing with a pop backing band. So I'm always cautious – a good quality world music artist – fantastic! Really representing the development of a tradition. World pop, I'm not particularly interested.

Her dissatisfaction at the way the show is understood in the wider sense is clear – the show, as any glance at its playlists will illustrate, does not limit itself to the repertoires perceived as belonging to 'World Music'. Furthermore her discomfort at this is echoed by the way that industry sometimes finds similar musical products presented – what she calls 'the Starbucks version', as familiar from advertising as from the music itself. The music becomes separated from its sources and becomes merely a signifier for the exotic or the expensive, the perceived authenticities of the music turned into leverage for capital. There is a high level of quality control at work here, and not just because there are only so many hours of airtime available. The market is a secondary or even tertiary consideration, behind issues of tradition and innovation; what is primary is this difficult-to-define notion of quality. That, of course, is not specific to any particular genre. Yet this willingness to move from style to style seems to represent both a virtue and a problem for the programme and how it is perceived.

The difficulty experienced by this kind of cross-genre broadcasting in finding a representative 'place' in the ranks of its own organisation reveals how genre-driven most music radio is, whether we are discussing American country music stations or the streamed domestic output of Radio 2. Yet Talkington asserts that, far from standing alone, the programme is central to and indicative of Radio 3's output as a whole, saying that 'it is the programme which grows out of the rest of Radio 3' and that *Late Junction* 'defines Radio 3 in terms of its output and quality'. This is a bold claim but one which, reflecting back upon the wide range of musical styles and content that the programme showcases, is firmly grounded in the evidence of the playlists, which serve as a kind of archive of influence. The audience can investigate and trace back through the lists how musical styles came to wider attention, and how the show has impacted upon the musical taste and 'scene' of any given period. Yet at any given moment, established listeners inevitably will fall away – satiated or repelled – while new ones, startled or intrigued, discover the show – so I wondered what kind of relationship the programme has with its audience.

PM: Do you know what the thresholds of tolerance are for the audience? How interactive is the programme?

FT: Well, I mentioned the outcry that greeted the Gavin Bryers, but we also got plenty saying 'yes this is what you should be doing'. Playing something a bit raucous that goes on a bit can upset people, there's no question about it, but often you'll hear 'I didn't like that piece but I'm glad you're playing it'. People who are in the spirit of the programme will definitely want you to play this kind of thing. In the early days when we were four nights a week and live every night we were completely interactive – they would e-mail in and we could start a conversation about your favourite guitarist, or something. Then in 2007 we went to three nights a week and started an hour later because the programme was then broadcast using the same system as is used through the night, so that stopped our immediate interactivity. We could still be in touch with people but there wasn't the same sense of immediacy. We still get lots of e-mails – people asking to hear something or commenting or asking where they can find a tune we've played. Once the playlists started being published on the website, you lost this sense of people writing in to ask what a certain track was and so on. So now we don't always know which pieces have aroused the most interest in any particular programme. In fact the playlists very often go up in advance of the programme, which I don't really like.

PM: Why is that done?

FT: There's evidence that some listeners like it to be like the other Radio 3 listings in the *Radio Times* so they can see who and what's coming on, but in a programme which is supposed to be beyond genres and about listening, I don't think they should go up until the show has been broadcast. It sounds a small thing but if you've planned one of these segues we were talking about, we want people to be enthralled by it, not to know that it's coming. But also you can look at the playlist in advance and if nothing leaps off the page, you might think 'Oh there's nothing on *Late Junction* tonight, I'm not going to listen'. Yet it's not about what it looks like on the page; there might be this amazing music waiting for you there, or that there might be the most wonderful voice you've ever heard on there.

The archival record represented by the playlists can, it seems, turn into something of a burden if published in advance – put simply, the element of surprise or the sublime and unexpected juxtapositions are somewhat reduced by advance notice and, moreover, by not hearing the show *as it happens*. This is what Fiona Talkington means when she speaks of 'the spirit of the programme', an ability to let connections flow and develop naturally: the Cesario Evora to Duke Ellington idea. As she notes, if the playlist doesn't immediately appeal then it might prove counterproductive to both listener and programme so that 'now we don't always know which pieces have aroused the most interest in any particular programme'. So if there is a kind of rise and fall in relative interactivity for the show, we might think about quite how, and where, the programme is listened to:

PM: So I suppose you are more dependent on less specific detail now – for example, do you know how the show is listened to – is it mainly via the iPlayer, or live, or via podcast?

FT: I couldn't quote the numbers at you but I do know that *Late Junction* is one of the most popular programmes on the iPlayer. It has a very, very loyal following, and because it's now on later, and people do have to go to bed and get up for work, we know that there are great numbers of people who hear the show the next day either on computers or iPad or wherever. People who love the show don't want to miss anything. We also get correspondence from around the world, so the iPlayer helps the show travel too. This makes a big difference.

PM: Is there a 'network' or equivalent shows, say, on public radio in the US or Australian or European stations?

FT: Well we hear that there are little pockets of similar programming – so you'll get stations in America who might play Norwegian music, say, on a show which gets an hour a week – often to serve communities with strong connections to the region they specialise in, so it's part of folk heritage and culture in those cases. But I've never heard of a programme that goes out three nights a week that covers such a huge range of music I don't think, no. Mixing this folk music, for want of a better term, mixed with Liszt or Schubert . . . it's the fact that it's on Radio 3 and there's an understanding of the music which makes it unique, I think.

The fact of having a globally unique piece of programming seems both a blessing and a source of confusion for the BBC; it has evolved naturally and without excessive editorial interference into a cultural showcase with few peers. The new technologies enable the show to be heard away from the traditional positions – by the radio set, at the appointed time as published in the *Radio Times* – and to travel round the world in a way that radio could never formerly have done. So the isolation is also a kind of opportunity to spread the idea of music programming that is willing to go beyond boundaries and is indeed frequently in active pursuit of such exploration. Given this kind of potential for a global reach, in every sense, the programme must seem a tempting platform for the music industry:

PM: What is the record industry's relationship with the show – from where do you get people pitching at you for a play on the programme?

FT: From all over the place – in fact often we are sent things which aren't particularly suitable for the programme, simply because some PR person will have been told 'Oh you've got to send it to *Late Junction*, they play all sorts of weird stuff', so you'll get a lot of indie or pop stuff, a lot of it really good, but just not right for the programme. Then you'll get the musicians themselves sending stuff in – there are a lot of brilliant singer-songwriters out there and that's great for music making but often they aren't right for the show or the sound quality of the recording isn't quite good enough, great voice, limited material, iffy voice, good songs and so on. Same with electronic – there's some fantastic material out there, but we can't play everything. Plus, we do have a limited amount of time on the programme, and we're not a charity shop – so to get on it has to be really good. We're back to the quality criteria again here. You hope the record companies will send the good stuff but sometimes they miss, and sometimes it's personal contact with musicians that brings it in – you find them rather than them pursuing you! Or you find stuff on your travels.

If we are to take John Peel and Charlie Gillett's shows as forerunners of the boldness of *Late Junction*, then both men had their favourites and ensured that the world knew about – say, the Fall and Dire Straits. In closing, I wondered who might owe their success in some way to *Late Junction*:

PM: Out of all the people you have discovered and played, is there one artist or album or musical style that *Late Junction* has really opened up to the world?

FT: As a genre it has to be Norwegian music, which would not be getting the airplay and audiences it does in this country if we hadn't played it; there are also bands like Sweet Billy Pilgrim who didn't have an album when I first started playing them. They just sent me some tracks, I loved them and played them and then a few years later they were nominated for a Mercury award. It wasn't just us, they needed plays on Radio 1 and 6 Music but you did hear them first on *Late Junction*. There are people whose profile has definitely been raised – Verity has done a lot for Chris Wood, for example, that made a difference for him. A young guy called Jono McLeery, who was flagged up to me by Tom Robinson, I love his stuff and play it and he's on the way now. It's not really anything I did, what musicians need is a package of support if they are going to succeed – unless it's a 'Terry Wogan discovers' type thing and has that massive exposure that the breakfast show gives you, of course. You're not going to reach number one just with a couple of plays on *Late Junction*, but it is going to help, and seep in and get to the right people. That's important.

Her estimations are undeniable – the likes of serene vocalist Solveig Slattahjell or the innovative Norwegian jazz trumpeter Arve Henriksson would not be filling the Royal Festival Hall had *Late Junction* not set the ball rolling for them – but she is also correct in her observation that a single show cannot alone make or sustain success for a chosen artist. Her reference to Terry Wogan picks up our Eva Cassidy example from elsewhere in this book and, as she notes, the artists needs a 'package of support'. This does not need to be completely industry driven – the kind of support in which radio simply rolls over and accepts the latest product on heavy rotation. That situation is, regrettably, commonplace and especially at the BBC. So the integrity *of Late Junction* is ever more valuable, rare and, as Fiona Talkington passionately asserts, it is important.

The specialist local music programme: *Down in the Grooves*, BBC Radio Leeds

James Addyman's show for BBC Radio Leeds, *Down in the Grooves*, is a very useful example of how the spaces between mainstream programming on BBC stations can be cultivated and made into a kind of permissive space in which non-mainstream and downright commercially invisible musics can be given airtime. The programme offers eclectic mixes of musical styles and eras – it also deviates from the Anglophone standardisation of mainstream music radio in that it often plays non-English language recordings, not in the *Late Junction* sense of pursuing that explicitly via World Music but, for example, Hungarian pop, Czech psychedelia or French 'Yeh Yeh' girl group tunes. The show began in 2004, at first in the 'small hours' slot after midnight where RAJAR figures no longer impinge upon programming. After building up a substantial following the show was moved to a 7–10 p.m. slot on a Thursday evening, broadcast live; it worked well here but, instructively, a change in management at Radio Leeds led to an emphasis on standardised, stranded programming in the evenings which left no room for the kind of wide-ranging eclecticism of *Down in the Grooves*. Thus it was moved back to a very late-night spot, which it still occupies, from 1 to 3 a.m. on Saturday mornings. Unsurprisingly, the show gets most of its listenership via the iPlayer in the following week – this, however, seems to suit the connoisseurial tone of the show – this is music to be discovered, played and replayed, and the new mediation of the iPlayer effectively delivers this capacity. Likewise the BBC Radio Leeds website publishes a playlist for the show so the listener may if they wish follow up anything they have heard and locate the source albums or singles. So the technology makes the potentially obscure musical track more rather than less accessible – instead of simply coming and going, it may be 'caught up with' in every sense – a sample playlist is reproduced in Appendix III. Unusually for local radio, the show is entirely an expression of its host's interests and enthusiasms, and I wondered how James Addyman came to find himself in such an unusually advantageous position, with such creative freedom in assembling his programmes.

PM: How did you begin working for the BBC in Leeds?
JA: I was working in Edinburgh as a DJ and got involved with student radio – we put in a proposal, it was accepted and a week later we were on air! So we thought 'we'd better start programming this'! On the evening the studio engineer would be there when we arrived, then he'd say 'OK, see you in two hours, I'm off to the pub'! So the show would reflect some of what we used to play in the clubs, and some other stuff we liked and just put it out there with no idea of who might be listening – so when people started phoning in and saying 'have you got this one?' and 'can you play this one?' and so on we were delighted and amazed.

So the show has its roots in DJ work as far as Addyman's own interest in playing music was concerned, and that is a traditional, if not the
only, route into music broadcasting; this, however, was allied to and
kick-started by engagement with that often overlooked field, student
radio. In such an environment free of playlists and over-prescriptive
regulation, the participants are granted a freedom of sorts to succeed
or fail or simply do the unexpected with little interference. In some
ways it is doubtful whether a show like this could develop from scratch
at a traditional, professionally inclined radio station; rather like the
indie label sector we have explored the real innovations tend to come
from the passions of the non-professional which then informs and
refreshes the mainstream output. So I wondered how the idea made
the leap from that free-form creativity of DJ'ing and student radio
programming to a BBC schedule.

PM: How did you then come to conceive of a show like *Down in
the Grooves*?

JA: When I first came down to Leeds as a BA [broadcasting
assistant] I worked almost non-stop at first, 72-hour weeks,
trying to get a foothold – the editor we had then was a 'small c'
conservative, and was very picky about who could go on air, and
what could go out on air. But in 2004 I got a full-time post and
that coincided with the arrival of a new station editor/manager
and he was more open to ideas – so I suggested something along
the lines of *Down in the Grooves* to him, which he gave the thumbs
up to, and then he left! That's how it goes in radio, but the new
guy came in and, to my surprise, thought it was a good idea
too – so we met and he said, right you'll be on air in September
[2004]! Which focused the mind. I wanted the show to be on in
this new spot from 1 a.m. as this was right at the start of when
the station went over to 24-hour broadcasting and also I knew it
would fit in with the online launch of the iPlayer, which I should
say wasn't completely new, as it had previously been called the
'Listen Again' platform.

So I knew that even if people didn't hear it on the air they
could catch up with it later – also this meant there was no pressure about listening figures as anything after 1 a.m. was not really
under pressure from RAJAR figures. Having said that it followed
Martin Kelner's late show which was very popular so *Down in the
Grooves* got very good figures and was even in the low end of the
RAJAR figures on occasion, which was unheard of! The slot gave
me the freedom to do exactly what I wanted to do which was to

play great stuff that people wouldn't otherwise get to hear, and
most likely wouldn't even get on the radio at all.

Addyman's desire for the show to go out in a slot traditionally considered the 'graveyard' slot of radio programming (1 a.m.) shows both
how different its aims were from conventional music programming
and also his understanding of the switch to 24-hour broadcasting
opening up fresh opportunities to increase the scope of what could go
out on air while still holding fast to the BBC's public service remit.
The RAJAR figures, as he notes, were less adaptable as by making
no record of listening figures between 1 and 6 a.m. on British radio,
they effectively embedded the notion that anything broadcast between
those hours would necessarily be of interest to only a minority listening audience. Thus the opportunity to put together a show which, it is
already assumed, very few people will be listening to effectively frees
the broadcaster from the usual industrial pressures, constraints and
limitations on content to which music radio programming is subject.
The broadcaster, in such circumstances, would seem to be free to play
whatever they chose. How then does a broadcaster approach such an
opportunity?

PM: Was the show always driven by your own interests and
     tastes?
JA: Oh yes, that was the whole idea really – I was very lucky! The
     show reflected my own interests, being made up of stuff I liked,
     stuff I'd found and stuff that was new – so I'd play Big Boss Man,
     for example, a Mod band who dwell in a kind of indeterminate
     moment of the 1960s, or some Rockabilly tune from an act from
     Folkestone or somewhere . . . I guess the point is that I'm not
     taking this music out of storage, it's a living breathing thing, not
     a museum piece that gets unwrapped, played then put back in
     the cupboard. Initially the show was part me playing the records
     and part interview, and once the show was given the green light
     I had my work cut out finding interviewees every week! So I got
     people I really wanted to talk to, like Ady Croasdell who is Head
     of Publishing at the Kent record label, and who ran the '6 T's
     Rhythm and Soul' night at the 100 Club in London which I think
     is the longest continuously running club night in the world, it's
     been running since 1979.
        Likewise Jonny Trunk who is one of the great living English
     eccentrics, and a joy to speak to – his show on Resonance
     FM is unmissable. Other people I interviewed included John

Schroeder (in-house producer at Pye in the 1960s), Electric Prunes drummer Preston Ritter, Gary Walker from the Walker Brothers, Colin Blunstone from the Zombies, Bruce Brand (drummer with the Milkshakes/Headcoats and a million other bands with Billy Childish), Gerald Short who is the main man behind the Jazzman reissue label, and Andy Votel and Dom Thomas from Finders Keepers Records. I spoke to Gary Walker in the States via one of the BBC's ISBN studios over there. Now, talking to these people was just brilliant but involved a heck of a lot of organising or running up and down the country to interview them. The show was always a pre-record so you could edit it all and make it sound good, but the live show on Thursdays was a different story!

A show like this, driven directly by the presenter's own tastes and enthusiasms, is very rare indeed. Long-running examples are limited and we return to Charlie Gillett's *Honky Tonk* shows in the 1970s for Radio London and, famously, John Peel's shows for BBC Radio 1 (1967–96) as forerunners. When the show was moved from the late night/early morning slot Addyman was happy to occupy, it was an index of the show's growing popularity but also necessitated substantive changes in the way the show was made and broadcast. Some of the freedoms offered by the non-RAJAR-assessed, connoisseurial timeslot were perhaps at risk of being lost once it was going out to a mid-evening, more numerous and more random listenership. I wondered how these changed imperatives impacted upon the show.

PM: What impact did the shift from the Thursday evening slot to the Saturday early morning time have on the way the show was constructed and listened to?

JA: Well that was year-long period when it went out live from 7 to 10 on Radio Leeds but with the last hour pre-recorded, usually an interview. The station manager called me in and told me it was moving from 1 a.m. to 7 p.m. on a Thursday – I was okay with it but not cock-a-hoop. The manager said 'You don't seem exactly thrilled' and I said 'well it's a different thing altogether now, are you sure you're not just throwing stuff at the wall to see what sticks?' But he believed in the show so we tried – it did well and was a whole other thing with listeners e-mailing and texting in all the time, making requests, asking for more information about the tunes they'd heard. It was great, but as I told the station manager, a different thing altogether. It ended up with less music on it too, funnily enough, because it fell into the daytime thing of reading out listener comments and requests.

Eventually moved back to late night, not because of figures but because of a change in BBC policy on 'Nations and Regions', when it was decided that notional listeners needed to be targeted and the key 'imagined listener' turned out to be a woman, whom the BBC management called 'Sue', who was supposed to be in her fifties. The slightly 'Boys Record Clubby' vibe of *Down in the Grooves* didn't really fit that, so back it went! I wasn't too upset about that really. It didn't really have any impact on the content I wouldn't say, but obviously the level of interactivity is different between a live show and a recorded one.

Clearly, the move from a marginal 'cult' slot to a more mainstream one brought at least as many restrictions on the shape and form of the show as advantages of bringing this music out into the light a little more and to the attention of a potentially larger audience. As Addyman notes, one of the changes was the issue of interactivity – making personal connections with the audience adds to the community dimension of the programme yet also slowed the internal dynamics of the show meaning that there was, paradoxically, less time for this rarely heard music to reach the airwaves as the audience take up more time praising it. So after this quick stint in the early evening was over and the late slot restored, I wondered if the show was – again like Peel or Gillett or indeed *Late Junction* – cherished if not quite fully understood by the station of which it forms an important part.

> *PM*: How is the show seen at the station – is it anomalous or is there a prescribed space in the schedules for a show not tied to promotion/playlists etc.?
>
> *JA*: I suppose the show fits in that it ticks a few boxes as far as management are concerned; it's certainly Reithian in that it seeks to educate and inform as well as entertain! There's so little room for anything other than mainstream music on radio now, and virtually nothing at all in the commercial sector, that it is tolerated, possibly even quite enjoyed by the people who make the decisions, even if they don't recognise most of what I play.

The show, perhaps oddly given its apparent 'left-field' categorisation, is indeed close to Lord Reith's original vision for the BBC as a body having the responsibility, even duty, to educate, inform and entertain. It could be argued that *Down in the Grooves* is able to do all three within the span of a two-minute obscure soul track from the mid-1960s. That point about content and recognition is a key one for a radio programme like this – regular listeners will perhaps 'expect the unexpected' but what could we say about are the fields and limits of the musical content of the show?

PM: What are the criteria for a *Down in the Grooves* track? What characterises the show's content?

JA: Well it has to be something with a great feel, a certain energy – not just anything in a given style, it must have a something extra, a great beat . . . an ability to surprise – I sometimes like to play obscure and unusual tracks by mainstream acts in order to show that these acts have more to them than might seem to be the case – so I'll play a Tom Jones track or even early Cliff Richard, or the B-sides by acts like Dave Dee Dozy Beaky Mick and Titch or the Tremeloes – it's great to have these acts sitting next to the 13th Floor Elevators or the Electric Prunes! So it might be French 'Yeh Yeh' music or it might be Fred Neil or Tim Buckley – filed as folk but there's so much going on once you hear it. But I suppose the show is best known for Northern Soul or Psych stuff. I also like strange cover versions – one that comes to mind is 'Jumpin' Jack Flash' by Ananda Shankar – an amazing noise, and you're 40 seconds into it before you'd ever even spot that it was that incredibly well-known Stones tune!

PM: Do you come under any external pressure to play or not play certain tracks or styles? Is everything on the show from your own collection?

JA: No pressure at all; station managers might look at the playlist on the website and recognise one name, but so long as they see that it gets decent listening or iPlayer figures and I show them the e-mails from all over the world from people who are enjoying the show online, then I suppose they're fine with it for now. I'd say 90 per cent of the stuff on the show is my own collection, vinyl mainly, and 10 per cent is what I pick out of what is sent to me – I get plenty of stuff sent through from the promo guys, but most of it is not what the show is about at all, so it's obvious they don't actually listen to it, but just see 'soul' or 'punk' on the webpage and go with that!

The connection between the cultural gatekeeping space of the DJ set and private record collection and the shared and open space of the radio show are clearly connected in this case. One is heavily informed by the other in a mutually responsive manner. The nature of a 'typical' *Down in the Grooves* track is clearly elusive and may well be something partly located outside of the recorded music itself – something on a coveted label, perhaps, or connected to a producer or studio. The deliberate pursuit of the non-digitised formats – playing vinyl records rather than files on a computer, the delivery mode of most mainstream music broadcasting in 2011 – is not merely anachronistic or clinging to old formats; rather, it is the only way that much of this music has survived. This of course connects back to the collection and the DJ set – a disc jockey needs, by definition, a collection of discs. This forms and informs the content of the programme in a way similar to but distinct from the contours of a 'live' DJ set in a club. I asked about the nature of this connection.

> *PM*: Is there an overlap between what you play on the show and your DJ work?
>
> *JA*: To a degree; but in a club the purpose is to get the room moving and let them dance – on the show I can include a whole range of material that probably wouldn't work in a club – sometimes I'll do a set in a bar and that's more of a mixture, you can get away with longer less rhythmic things, more head-nodding. But in a club you need to keep them working! Talking about great records from unexpected places, I've been known to play the Ventures' [late 1950s guitar instrumental group best remembered for their version of 'Walk Don't Run'] version of 'Louie Louie' in a club, it always works brilliantly, it's so primal and has got the beat, the riff, the energy. People would say 'The *Ventures*'? But it never misses. Likewise Cliff Richard, his 'Dynamite' is brilliant as is his version of 'The Girl Can't Help It' and people can never quite believe it when I tell them who the artist is.

Herein is one of the key differences between the same tune on the radio and in a club – no back-announcements or context are required in the club, just those key elements – 'the beat, the riff, the energy'. The same three minutes of music is mediated differently by the club DJ, the space in which it is heard and the audience who respond to it. On the radio, that tune is experienced individually, in different places and even, via the iPlayer, at different times, where it also might be stopped and started or listened to over and over again. Furthermore, the radio audience is diffuse whereas the club audience is a single entity which has a will – do they dance or not? – but which may be overcome by stealth: 'people can never quite believe it when I tell them who the artist is'. So in all this who might we say the show is 'for'?

PM: In your estimation, is there a 'typical' listener to the show? What kind of relationship does the show have with its audience?

JA: Well from the e-mails I get, I've found that the youngest listener is about 20, and the oldest 72! There is, I suppose, a record collector element to the audience but also people who are just interested in music, maybe they like hearing the stuff they know from their youth if it's 50s or 60s music, maybe it's stuff they don't know even if they were there at the time, some are young people to whom it's all new, and others who aren't so bothered about the historical context and just like the mix of sounds they'll hear! I get lots of e-mails from people saying what they enjoy about the show, and the music; one guy e-mailed to say he works on a rig in Yemen, and has the show blasting out as he works! I like the thought of Yemeni goatherds hearing the 13th Floor Elevators and me yakking away alongside them, out there in the desert somewhere! I get a range of messages from all over the world, Croatia, Canada, New Zealand, Holland, it's amazing. Plus the show has a strong link with the local scene as well, so I can plug events like, say, at the HiFi Club in Leeds or an all-nighter in Brighouse. I sometimes wonder if Brighouse sounds exotic to the person listening in Croatia! Sometimes guys who were in bands Google themselves and find via the online playlists that I've been playing tracks from their bands and get in touch with me and say 'Oh, I've got this bit of film or these live tapes do you want a copy' and of course I say 'yes please!' Of course, I do my own DJ sets too, but I tend not to plug those directly on the show.

This characterises the reach of the show very well indeed. There is a substantial age range – itself unusual in the increasingly homogenised and stranded radioscape – and it creates a community of expertise around the music which draws together disparate individuals who would perhaps have little in common otherwise. It serves the local function – with plugs for the themed nights or DJ sets at local clubs, five minutes' walk from the BBC Radio Leeds studio in the case of the estimable HiFi Club. Yet thanks to the Internet – a fresh field of mediation for this music – the local becomes the global, the tight-knit community of experts, collectors and enthusiasts becomes a world-wide group, and paradigms of exoticism and charm pinpointed by the likes of Said in his *Orientalism* (1978) are polarised, driving Addyman's speculation about the 13th Floor Elevators being heard by Yemeni shepherds and the local transforming into the object of desire in the distant mind's eye thanks to the medium of the show: 'I sometimes wonder if Brighouse sounds exotic to the person listening in Croatia!'

Given the show's global reach – both real and potential – I wondered if James Addyman saw *Down in the Grooves* as part of a 'wave' of similar endeavours, connecting independent ideas and projects into a bigger social network of musical connoisseurship?

> *PM*:   Do you feel that the show has any peers on other radio stations, national, 'local' or online, making a network and providing this kind of listening to the dedicated, connoisseurial listener? It always seems curious to me that the people who are most enthusiastic and informed about popular music are the least-well served by standard music radio programming.
>
> *JA*:   I couldn't agree more. There were a few others doing similar things, such as Vic Galloway in Glasgow and Mary Fox in Stoke, although her show is gone now. They mixed brand new, unsigned and also classic Northern Soul and pop, well known and obscure. That's a bit of what *Down in the Grooves* does, I suppose. The absence of this kind of thing on radio, whether you're talking about local, national or commercial providers, was one of the key reasons why I started buying records in the 1980s as the stuff that was on the radio was just not what moved or interested me. As I said there are other shows around, regional stations sometimes do have these home-grown one-offs, rather than it being a policy decision to 'create' one. There's nothing 'West Yorkshire' about *Down in the Grooves* although of course the local scene features in the listings and events sense – but the music can come from anywhere – and usually does. The saving of '6 Music' [after an extensive online campaign] shows that there is a constituency out there for the non-mainstream and the uncommercial sounds, and online stations may well be the way forward. However, there are always funding issues about these stations so a station like Resonance FM is often running fundraising events and campaigns.

While correctly noting that the show is not 'West Yorkshire' in its musical repertoires it provides an information exchange about club nights, gigs and record fairs. He connects the successful campaign to 'save' the BBC's digital station 6 Music from closure in 2010 to the hidden audience for non-mainstream music radio programming yet also notes that when these shows do emerge on local rather than national stations it is often the product of happy accident rather than corporate policy as was the case with BBC 6 Music. These 'home-grown one-offs' have less funding and less ability to attract the big name DJs that jostle for space on 6 Music but they are also to some extent free from the pressures that were brought to bear upon that station and led to the threat of closure. Increasingly, public service radio is having to behave like commercial radio – money is the key issue. The BBC cannot advertise, relying on the licence fee alone to fund their output. This will inevitably put minority interest music, be that 1960s soul and psychedelia or Radio 3's more eclectic output, under the spotlight as costs are assessed. The election in 2010 of a government in the UK which is broadly hostile to state-funded broad-casting and heavily supportive of the kind of commercial concern char-acterised by News International has made these pressures even more acute. To conclude I asked James Addyman how he saw the future of music radio in the UK developing, given these conditions, and his reply was somewhat vexed.

PM: How do you see UK music radio going in the next ten years or so? Will it become more or less amenable to a show like *Down in the Grooves* – that is, will eclectic individuality be encouraged or will homogenous content (like the 2010 model of the Capital Radio brand being rolled out of London to 'local' providers) increasingly be the dominant mode?

JA: Well this is an area of great dispute. Commercial radio? No chance. There's no room for anything like this on commercial radio; it's the opposite, with content becoming increasingly more narrow and homogenised. There's actually a big fight going on and it's going on right now – I love that Jeremy Paxman can get Mark Thompson on and make him squirm – compare this with Sky 'News', and I use the term amusedly, with Adam Boulton and Kay Burley making excuses for News International non-stop. Can you imagine them giving Rupert Murdoch a hard time in an interview? Never.

There are plenty of people in the Conservative/LibDem Coalition government and in the right-wing papers who would love to stamp out the BBC – they use a bit of the Murdoch rhetoric 'oh we just want the BBC scaled back a bit' but it's clear they want the field to themselves. It's empire building à la Milton Friedman – they're OK until another empire wants a bit of their empire! So radio is at the front line of all that, and it's absolutely vital that we keep allowing the obscure and the unusual on the air. I was disappointed that Bruce Dickenson's show was kicked off 6 Music for example, not that I like heavy metal, I can't stand it in fact, but it is very popular and there was a big audience for that show. The roots of that show went right back to Alan Freeman on a Saturday afternoon (BBC Radio 1 1973–8, 1989–93) and Tommy Vance's *Friday Rock Show* (BBC Radio 1 1978–93). Like John Peel's shows – who is now revered like a saint but when he was actually still at Radio 1 they treated his show terribly, moving it all over the schedules toward the end – these things have always only ever been tolerated and when they are got rid of, it's never to do with listener figures and everything to do with policy or change at the top. Peel was the place to go for all types of music, not just punk and so on, so you'd hear one tune and think 'what on earth is THAT' and then the next record would be the greatest thing you ever heard. That just will not happen on a commercial network. That's why the BBC is worth protecting.

In these final thoughts James Addyman expresses the anxieties of the public service broadcaster not only for their little plot of a couple of hours on the radio each week but for the soul of broadcasting itself. By using the example of the minority interest music show he makes the point that to abandon such provision is to surrender the purpose of music radio altogether to commercial concerns. This, he argues, is embodied, if imperfectly, by the BBC and thus it is important that the kind of mediated space offered by a programme like *Down in the Grooves* – expert, informed and connoisseurial but also wholly democratic and open – persists as evidence of the spirit of what he called the Reithian remit of education, information and entertainment. That is indeed worth protecting.

Radio

1. What is the place and role of 'niche' music radio in contemporary broadcasting in the public and commercial sectors?
2. Look at the schedules for your local BBC and commercial radio stations – what scope is there for specialist music programming?
3. Find out how and why BBC 6 Music was 'saved' by a consumer campaign in 2010.
4. Can music programming ever be truly 'local' and 'specialist' in the digital era?

5 State of Independence? The Independent Record Label as Mediator of Popular Music

Introduction

> 'Independence ain't dependence' (Gang of Four, 'Independence')

In some ways to discuss the 'independent' record label is in itself a misnomer as in the early days of recording all record production was 'independent', operating out of private studios and issuing recordings on their own labels in the local area. This is seen to comic effect in Joel Coen's *O Brother Where Art Thou* (1999), where in a key scene the escaped convicts earn some dollars by going to a small recording studio where, they have heard, 'a man pays good money for you to sing into a can'. The song they record, the American traditional tune 'Man of Constant Sorrow' becomes a huge success, being sold in independent music stores throughout the southern US thanks to the new popularising medium of radio. That all of a sudden there was a much wider demand for a single recording demonstrates the roots of the centralised model of the music industry – instead of a great number of scattered, individual producers, shifts in consumer demand (in the movie's case, for a single recording) pushed these separate businesses together the better to make and distribute the product that is in demand. This is why legendary artists such as Robert Johnson or Charley Patton had such disparate and patchy recorded catalogues – they would simply record for any man who give them money to sing into a can, wherever their itinerant blues lives took them along the road, and then that studio would press up and sell the discs locally – this is also why there are several different recordings by the likes of Johnson or Patton of the same songs; they were re-recorded to meet local demand or interest as record players became more affordable and the reach of radio spread further and further across the US. Likewise these labels, attached to studios, provided a jumping-off point for the new record industry after the Second World War. Famously Sun Records in Memphis, owned by Sam Phillips, was an independent record label and recording studio, through the doors of which came many significant names of American music – the so called 'Million Dollar Quartet' of Johnny Cash, Jerry Lee Lewis, Carl Perkins and Elvis Presley all started out at Sun, for example.

Independent (or 'indie') record labels fell out of favour in the 1950s rock and roll era and then into the boom period for pop of the 1960s, as they came to be seen as little more than stables for talent which the 'major' record companies could come and cherry pick from, in the way that RCA Victor had plucked Elvis Presley from Sun. Independent labels rarely had their acts under any kind of legally enforceable contract so this kind of route from indie to major quickly became the industry standard. Curiously, while Factory Records of Manchester, perhaps the most famous of all UK independent labels of the recent era, had a similar 'no contracts' policy, most acts, however, chose to stay with the label. As Nice (2011) notes, this may well have been because the lack of contractual obligation was symbolic of a wider sense of creative freedom offered by the label which simply would not have existed at a major. Factory came out of the post-punk cultural landscape and, as with much else in popular culture, punk proved the watershed for the independent record label. However, it's worth remembering that the best known punk acts such as the Sex Pistols and the Clash never recorded for independent labels – the former signed to that bastion of the British music industry establishment EMI (skitting the cover of the Beatles' first album for an early promotional picture in the process) and the Clash signed up to CBS, the UK arm of Columbia. It was the young less well-placed bands that followed in the wake of acts like these that needed a quick and effective outlet for their music – recorded quickly, issued fast, on to the next one – and the revelation that anyone could make and issue a record for a modest sum became the business corollary to the 'anyone can do it' three-chord aesthetic of the music itself. So when in Manchester, the young band Buzzcocks decided to make their own record they pushed the door open for hundreds of similarly minded new groups to do the same. Pete Shelley of Buzzcocks recalled that 'We made our own record only because we found out that we could! You didn't have to wait for EMI or RCA or whoever it was to notice you. So it cost I think £500 for 1,000 copies, pressed up, picture sleeve, and if you sold only half of them at £1 each you'd still be okay and have the music out there' (*Dancing In the Street*, BBC 1998). The hidden door into the music business had been unlocked and the 'workers' could, in some small way, take back the means of production by recording, designing, pressing, distributing and selling their own work through independent record shops across the UK.

The commercial success of any music depends upon proper marketing and distribution and in the pre-Internet era this meant getting product to record shops – in Leeds this meant 'Jumbo Records', in Manchester 'Piccadilly', in Liverpool 'Probe', in Newcastle 'Volume', in York 'Red Rhino'. These all became subcultural hubs in their own right. Despite the regional nature of this phenomenon, the independent label business still remained centred in London, at the Rough Trade organisation in Notting Hill run by Geoff Travis. He would later create a distribution network for UK and worldwide independent record shops which was called, with some irony, 'the Cartel'. As recorded by Taylor (2010) the Cartel crashed badly in the early 1990s, taking a lot of shops and labels down with it, although the Rough Trade label and shops survived. So the new creativity – or rather the new ability to make and distribute recorded music – found a corresponding marketplace in the independent record shops. The mainstream and independent music industries ran parallel for some years with occasional crossovers from one to the other – Buzzcocks were themselves one of the first to make this jump from their own New Hormones record label, which had issued their famous *Spiral Scratch* debut EP in late 1976, to join the punk roster at United Artists, the company started in Hollywood by Charlie Chaplin and Mary Pickford in 1919, so in its roots a film indie in its own right.

Often, however music that emerged on independent labels was simply not built for the major labels, whether it be too uncompromisingly radical in its aesthetic like Throbbing Gristle (see Ford 1999) or as politically sensitive as early singles by Northern Irish band Stiff Little Fingers such as 'Suspect Device' and 'Alternative Ulster'. Thus music which the majors would never have touched found its way to market via independent labels and record shops. While Throbbing Gristle never fully commercialised their sound, 'SLF' soon signed to Chrysalis within a year of their 1979 debut album and became a surprisingly slick and efficient mainstream rock band (see Link 2009). This is the risk for both band and label when an act jumps from indie to major – the band may find their work compromised, and the edge for which the label signed them may be smoothed away and their commercial appeal reduced as a consequence.

Partly in response to this perceived dilution of power and potential a second wave of better organised and more fiercely independent labels grew up in the very late 1970s and early 1980s – more than three years after the original wave – focusing again on localised cultural and geographical centres. Thus Manchester became dominated by Factory run by local newsreader and cultural entrepreneur Tony Wilson,

Liverpool by Zoo run by Bill Drummond who would later achieve massive pop success himself as half of the KLF. Similarly Glasgow was best known for Postcard, Bristol for Subway and so on. These labels again provided access for local bands seeking to get a start in the industry without having to pay homage to the majors in London but, paradoxically, these labels began to be seen as a kind of 'major' in those areas with smaller concerns considered less significant. So bands would feel the need to send their demos to Factory or Postcard, just like they would to the Artist & Repertoire departments at EMI or CBS in London. As bands on these labels became established and successful – Joy Division, the Durutti Column on Factory, the Teardrop Explodes and Echo and the Bunnymen on Zoo, Orange Juice and Aztec Camera on Postcard – these dynamics only increased. Despite the desirability of these prestige independents, of the acts named here only the Factory bands stayed with their indie label, all four others signing quickly to London majors.

This characterises a key aspect of the traditional dynamic between 'major' and 'independent' labels – the indies have traditionally discovered and given early developmental space to acts who, after some success and the establishment of reputation and style, are bought up by the larger labels which are able to provide more robust promotional and marketing networks and budgets. It was not until the arrival of bands like the Smiths at Rough Trade and Cocteau Twins at 4AD, both in 1983, that a situation arose where an act could be commercially very successful and also be retained by their original parent label. The commercial returns on the success of such acts enabled their parent labels to grow and foster other talent. Equally key was the support of other media and programmes like John Peel's BBC show became extremely important as a place to hear and be heard, while the weekly music press competed with each other to discover the 'next big thing'. So did punk create the independent sector or did that sector facilitate punk? This is hard to answer because there is, unsurprisingly, no single definitive version of how the two elements arose and colluded – what we might say is that punk might not have happened in the way it did if it hadn't been for the local economies, both cultural and political, which were characterised by the independent recording industry, studios and commercial outlets.

What then is 'independent' music? Is it part of the sound or is it a spirit felt within the music? Where is the evidence located? Initially this was found in the publishing of 'independent' charts. They were necessary to record the rising sales in music that would not come anywhere near the 'official' charts which were then compiled according to sales return figures from what were called 'Chart Return Shops'. These were unlikely to stock records that fell outside the remits of the major labels, so the sales of independent labels were effectively invisible. Now, as Steve Rusby and Ben Watt note in our case studies, the independent record label is almost as old as the mechanised production of music itself but what was different in the punk and post-punk periods is that there was a degree of organisation, initially via the Cartel, which enabled a kind of alternative market to develop and flourish, making the 'official' charts and record stores seem out of date and out of touch with what was really happening in British popular music at the time.

The first independent chart did not appear, as one might expect, in the *NME* but in the 'rock' weekly paper *Sounds*. The debut list appeared in the issue published on 19 January 1980 and was partially driven by their interest in and promotion of a wave of young rock acts the paper dubbed the 'New Wave of British Heavy Metal'. These bands, which included Def Leppard from Sheffield and Iron Maiden from East London, were following the examples of their older punk siblings and making their own records. This was particularly intriguing because heavy metal had been seen to be the epitome of the old bloated music industry model that punk had been minded to overthrow – Led Zeppelin, Black Sabbath and Uriah Heep, for example. This 'New Wave of British Heavy Metal' prompted *Sounds* to publish this independent labels chart and what became clear was that while punk and rock music dominated the rankings, all forms of music would appear – it would depend on how the records were pressed and distributed rather than their musical content. So, as Lazell (2000) recorded, a big selling country song or folk song or even a spoken word record would appear in the 'independent' chart if it did not appear on a major label. Sometimes, as in the case of the Smiths and the Cocteau Twins, the top single of the independent chart would also feature in the 'official' Top 40 as shown on *Top of the Pops*, the then all-powerful force in making chart music visible on television. With this kind of expanded definition of the term, amusing anomalies in demarcation can occur – for example both Paul McCartney and Kylie Minogue could be categorised as indie acts as both have had recordings issued by independent labels. Although neither 'official' or 'indie' chart is particularly significant in the marketplace at present, it still indexes where musical creativity is presently best seen, according to genre, individual artists or geographical location.

What is more significant is that 'independent' shortened to 'indie' has changed its meaning – it is now descriptive of a sound or a style, in the same way that one might see 'jazz' or 'blues' or electronica' on the browsers of your online or local record store. 'Indie' has come to connote a recognisable musical style just as strongly as it does an approach or an 'attitude' and no longer refers solely to the means via which the music is made. It has become a marketing term, carrying with it some, if not all, of the positive associations of 'authenticity' that the initial independents earned for the term.

Changes in recording technologies have also complicated the termi-nology. The great Canadian artist Jane Siberry followed the lapsing of her contract with Warner Brothers in the mid-1990s not by renegotia-tion but, discerning that the music business was changing fast, set up her own label, Sheeba. Siberry was practising 'customer-led pricing' via the Sheeba website long before more famous exponents of the idea such as Radiohead tried it. After uploading her back catalogue, bought out from Warners, she allowed customers to pay a 99 cent charge per track, download full albums for $7 or download tracks for free which would be described at the virtual checkout as 'A gift from the artist'. On 23 April 2010 I asked her about this policy and whether she was happy that she had taken this path:

> Yes I am happy because it set the music free. I call it passing it forward. People can hear it, pass it on, spread it around, that's what I wanted and what I still want. Or would like, seeing as it's not up to me.

This policy was followed, indirectly, by a series of albums part-funded by donations from her fan base and her 2010 'Salon World Tour' during which she avoided the conventions of the music industry alto-gether by inviting her admirers around the world to set up shows in their homes or small venues, or 'Salons', where she would come and play, negotiating fees and expenses with each 'host' individually. It was a remarkable success, running from January to June 2010, enabling her to play nearly 100 shows from her hometown of Vancouver in Canada and the US, via Pudsey West Yorkshire, in England, Scandinavia, continental Europe and then across Australia and New Zealand. So in this case being an 'independent' artist means something more than the manner of distribution for an album. As Gang of Four noted in the last line of their last album *Hard* in 1984: 'independence ain't dependence'.

Receiving more media coverage, Radiohead's 2009 album *In Rainbows* was initially released on the band's website and was subject to customer set pricing similar to that pioneered by Jane Siberry – that is, consumers could pay one penny or one hundred pounds, or indeed nothing at all to download the album. They found that roughly only a third of downloaders took advantage of the opportunity to get the album for nothing, with the majority paying between £4 and £20. Band vocalist Thom Yorke told *Time* magazine that

> I like the people at our record company, but the time is at hand when you have to ask why anyone needs one. And, yes, it probably would give us some perverse pleasure to say 'Fuck you' to this – decaying business model.

This idea of a decaying business model is precisely what concerns us here. While working at different levels of the industry – Radiohead play stadia, Jane Siberry plays your front room if you ask her nicely – both are seeking to reconfigure the business model upon which the music industry has run for decades.

So, bearing this in mind, the following case studies examine how that state of independence can be both problem and opportunity for music and musicians and to what degree a record company can function independently while still operating efficiently within the music industry of which it is part.

Case study I: Buzzin' Fly Records

Our first case study looks at the London-based independent label Buzzin' Fly, which deals mainly, but not exclusively, in electronic dance music. It was started by and is run and owned by Ben Watt.

Watt comes from a very musical family, with his father Tommy Watt being a renowned big band leader throughout the 150s and 160s. Both he and his wife and musical partner Tracey Thorn were signed to London-based indie Cherry Red as solo artists, with Thorn also being a member of trio the Marine Girls. Between them they had already released half a dozen albums, EPs and singles before they linked up at the University of Hull, where they were both students. In 1982 the pair formed Everything but the Girl, which had a recording career stretching over nearly two decades. In that time their music to some extent described the arc of how the industry changed and developed in parallel with the new media technologies: their first release was a three-track 45 for Cherry Red, the A-side being a cover of Cole Porter's 'Night and Day', and their last, to date, a remix anthology called *Adapt or Die*.

Everything but the Girl's music was strong and fragile, stable and ever-changing. Thorn's serenely expressive voice provided a perfect setting for lyrics which brimmed with wit, candour and a particularly feminised intelligence. This was well matched by Watt's substantial musicality and his powerful gift for melody, harmony and arrangement.

Over fifteen years, they issued ten albums which displayed these distinctive features, yet what was most remarkable about the work as a whole was its creative restlessness. This brought a musical eclecticism ranging from 'indie' to Jim Webb-style epic country pop, studied minimalism to soul revues, acoustic singer-songwriter intimacies tunes to thunderous, globe-shakingly successful electro dance pop. Each album took a different musical path and the group are rarely given credit for this deep and wide musicality. A serious illness which befell Ben Watt in 1992 forced the pair to focus on other matters than music, a period captured in Watt's candid 1997 memoir *Patient*.

After he was restored to health, a collaboration with Massive Attack on their 1994 album *Protection* led them into electronic 'dance' music with much success, including the global mid-1990s success of 'Missing' in a Todd Terry remix and the *Walking Wounded* album. The next few years involved much touring, shows where the balancing act between the group's acoustic roots and their new electronic style was deftly handled. What was notable was that the 'new' style still emphasised the crafted song alongside the rhythmic element. The *Temperamental* album of 1999 continued this pathway, with less commercial success, but by this time Watt had already begun to work as a producer and DJ, beginning with a track called 'Lone Cat'. Recorded for his own pleasure, it broke out and proved remarkably successful on the London and New York club scenes; this persuaded him to set up a record company to market such music, which he called Buzzin' Fly. The name comes from a Tim Buckley tune, smartly linking this electronic music with his acoustic roots. The label is renowned for the high quality of its catalogue and the aesthetic of its packaging and promotional ephemera, alongside the bold mixtures of acoustic and electronic textures which typify the label's musical identity. Buzzin' Fly also runs club nights worldwide. It is a most unusual and highly individualised variant on the independent model. I spoke to Ben Watt about how he came to set up the label, his experiences of running an independent niche genre label and his feelings about the future of independent music production.

> *PM*:   How did the idea for Buzzin' Fly first come about and how did you go about setting it up?
>
> *BW*:   Well it probably goes back to the life I lived as a teenager, in the heady days of post-punk, when it was suddenly made apparent that you didn't have to be in Yes or Pink Floyd to be in a band. Punk blew the doors off and let everyone have a go. Certainly for our generation it was very exotic and intoxicat-

ing, the idea that you could do it yourself – have a band and join an independent label. I think at the time I was, like a lot of people, very into the whole aesthetic of labels, not just the music that they put out. In particular people like Peter Saville at Factory, that idea of a stable, an identity, that was very strong.

Then I think, scrolling forward, Everything but the Girl had reached a kind of pinnacle of success in the late 1990s and we'd toured a the world with *Walking Wounded*, and I really felt I'd got to the end . . . I'd climbed a hill and reached the top a bit with mainstream pop, and I wanted to go back and rediscover something a bit rootsier again. I'd been wrapped up in the dance and electronic scene of the mid-1990s, and decided a route back in would be through DJ'ing and underground clubs, which was something I'd never really experienced before, and I hooked up with Jay Hannon who was the buyer of House Music at Black Market, which was this hotbed of 12" singles and underground stuff in London. So we set up this club night called Lazy Dog and initially we just played every other Sunday in West London and built up this following . . . I didn't really have any intention of starting a label, but the crunch came when I actually made a track myself in my own studio to play specifically at the club, took it down on the Sunday night, I'd just made an acetate of it to play at the club – this was mid-1990s, before burning your own CDs of course – played it in the club and there was a phenomenal response. It only takes seven or eight people to come up in a club and ask what a track is, and that's enough, you know that it's a hot track . . . the dance floor responds. I was really thrilled! I'd made this thing entirely by myself. So I pressed up fifty copies on white labels, sent them out to a few DJ friends and thought nothing of it – you know, that was the only use for it – but then I got a phone call from New York from a friend who ran a record shop in Manhattan saying 'Is this you?' He played a bit down the phone and it was my track; I thought 'what the . . .?' What had happened is that someone had got hold of one of the fifty copies I'd given out to friends, and they'd bootlegged it, and suddenly 1,500 copies were all over the dance music scene in New York. I was extremely flattered but felt this was just going too far. I managed to find the distributor who was doing it and I struck a deal with them, so that if they stopped pumping them out, I'd send them some more and they could sell those instead. And that really was how Buzzin' Fly started

because I thought if I'm going to do this, and it's a hot track, I
might as well just put it out.

PM: So which of the early ones was this?

BW: This was 'Lone Cat' – that was the first one I did this way.
So as soon as I'd made the decision, all that stuff I mentioned
earlier – the punk thing, the aesthetic of it – started to flood
into the equation. I wanted the label to be graphically interesting, aesthetic and House music didn't really have those sort of
parameters, you tend to get a die-cut 12" bag, stick the disc in it
and that was it.

PM: It was more utilitarian in its presentation and its use, wasn't
it

BW: That's right, exactly; Mo'wax, James Lavelle's label, were
one of the first to start putting out underground hip-hop and
electronic music in an aesthetically considered sleeve. Then
people started using reverse board rather than the shiny side,
people started to become aware of how it could look great in
itself at that underground dance level and that's what I wanted
Buzzin' Fly to have . . . you know, a little world about it, nice
website, great graphic design, you were buying into an ethos.

Watt links the aesthetic and artistic dynamics of the label back in
the explosion of independent musical production in the mid to late
1970s, the moment that a new generation saw that, in the vernacular,
anyone could do it – make a record, press, design and distribute under
their own steam and according to their own desires, and not those of
a parent company. Likewise that independent production pre-dated
the now commonplace technique of burning one's own CDs for
promotional, sale and distribution, effectively replacing the inferior
copying offered by analogue cassette tapes (the former method of
sending one's music to interested parties) with an exact digital copy
of the finished work. Yet we note too that he took as his model not
the rudimentary elements of DIY culture – the xeroxed A4 sheet, the
rough edges connoting authenticity – on the contrary his models, such
as Peter Saville at Factory or 23 Envelope who designed the very characteristic and ornate sleeves for 4AD were deliberately aiming high
in terms of design and art value – to cite a renowned and infamous
example, the 'floppy disc' sleeve for New Order's original 12" single
of 'Blue Monday' was so costly and complex to produce that Factory
lost money on each copy sold (see Nice 2011). This kind of cavalier
approach to creativity is treasurable but brings with it an unsteady and
uncertain future for any company that practises it, so I wondered what

Ben Watt felt about having seen the business from both within and without such processes.

> PM: To go back a bit, what if anything from your experience as a musician signed to independent labels, such as Cherry Red, has informed your running of one?
>
> BW: Well the luxury I had was having had the experience of both worlds. As you say I have a very soft spot for my early days hanging out at the Cherry Red offices, I just thought it was fantastic! Then later I experienced the sheer profit and loss side of putting records out via the major labels, and all the campaigns you have to put together, right from pressing, manufacture, marketing, promotion, distribution . . . I saw how it was done and saw how a lot of money could get wasted. So when it came to setting up Buzzin' Fly, I think I knew the structure of how to put records out, but I wanted to do it in a much more prudent way, where there was good housekeeping right from the beginning, so it was going to be like a microcosmic version of what I'd learned on bigger labels, I suppose. We spent a lot of time setting up the office, going round the second-hand shops just buying up nice stuff for the office, so everyone had a nice environment – books, old furniture . . . just somewhere nice to be rather than something cold and corporate, so everyone felt that they were part of this world of music and enthusiasm.

This combination of a musician's enthusiasm and quietly acquired business acumen makes for an unusual and potent combination in label management. This idea of 'good housekeeping' is the coming together of these two elements, with the great advantage of starting, as Watt says, 'from scratch' without the embedded infrastructure which renders internal change difficult for long-established and very large record companies. EMI's problems with dealing with the new marketplace realities are examined by Paul Williams, editor of *Music Week*, elsewhere in this book and are a model of what can happen to an organisation of such a scale if the ground shifts under the industry's feet. Working at this scale enables an identity to be created too, with the business environment being reflective of a set of ethical and aesthetic criteria. This is different, however, from what we will discover in the case of Pure Records in that there it is effectively a family business, whereas Ben Watt needed to recruit good people from where he could – the Rusbys' extended family principle means that all is kept in-house in every sense. Again, unlike Pure, Buzzin' Fly could not rely on the sales of one act to sustain it, not even its founder. I asked how the label went on to the next stage of development.

PM: At what stage did the label develop beyond being an outlet for your own stuff?

BW: At Lazy Dog so many tracks passed under your nose from people who were making stuff that just never came out, you'd think this is such a waste. Those sorts of things used to frustrate me, and I thought if you had a better structure and a bit of marketing intelligence, and a little bit of money, then you could make something out of this. So it was for my first few signings. There was a track, that by Rodamaal, 'Love Island', on a tiny French label called Jazzup, we played it to death at Lazy Dog and another night we did at Notting Hill Arts Club, and made a big success of it. No other DJs were playing it because no one else could get hold of copies. So I contacted them in France saying 'I love this stuff have you got any more?'

I kind of struck gold because it turned out that Rodamaal was made up of four different people – Rocco, the Ro part, then Da was Davide, who left shortly afterwards, Maal was Manou and Alex – and they were all brilliant DJs and producers in their own right who lived in Lyon, one lived in Lisbon. They sent me another tune 'Musica Feliz' straight away and I asked if I could sign it and that became the second release on Buzzin' Fly. Manou still puts stuff out now on the label, as does Rocco, separately. As Rocco said to me, they would still just be bumping along the bottom if I hadn't reached in and fished them out, because they were just local French DJs . . . so it's great to be able to give people that sort of opportunity really.

PM: So you are in a position where you can issue what you like, rather than a mix of what you like and focusing on what you know will sell in order to subsidise the stuff you like?

BW: We're a step away from that model, definitely. We shouldn't gloss over the fact that I have the ability to be something of a benefactor for Buzzin' Fly because of my financial security, but having said that it was clear from the very beginning that I wanted Buzzin' Fly to stand on its own two feet, I didn't want it to just be like a vanity publishing thing. So we do run a really tight ship and although a lot of the time it's a breakeven business it just about keeps itself going and I don't have to pump too much of my own money into it. I do try and sign tracks that will turn a small profit every time; I don't just sign tracks I love, I sign ones that I also think other DJs will love and that will do well in clubland.

This combination of pragmatism and enthusiasm for the music would seem to be a prerequisite for running an independent label, of course, but as Ben Watt notes few 'start-up' labels are in the position of having such a financially secure base. His experience of working with, and sometimes against or in spite of, prescribed budgets within the indie sector and at the peak of mainstream commercial success enabled him to bring well-tempered industry insight as well as financial backing to the project. Dance music is often credited with having 'saved' vinyl in the initial rush to digital via compact disc and other less successful digital formats but I wondered, in the new digital realities of the music marketplace where the music is increasingly not required to have any physical format at all, how he saw Buzzin' Fly pressing on from its present position:

PM: Buzzin' Fly has to some extent thrived partly because you know and understand the music from the inside, as a musician as well as a record company boss which isn't always the case, as we know . . .

BW: Yes, and it's very much harder now than it was, say, five years ago . . . the market is absolutely saturated with digital labels with very low overheads who don't even press up vinyl anymore, there's almost no cost involved in the production, because it's all made by producers at home on laptops and the distribution is zero because there's no manufacturing involved. This is driving quality down, and it's extremely competitive – we're suffering as a result, and that's one of the downsides of this kind of digital revolution, everyone says 'oh it's a level playing field for everybody' and that's certainly true but when costs come down so often quality does too.

PM: But Buzzin' Fly will keep producing the physical object, the vinyl record?

BW: We have a hardcore who are collectors and I think it'll bottom out somewhere around 500 copies, that's my informed guess, which is just about enough to make it worth doing. In the heady days you might sell 6–7,000 – 'Lone Cat' sold 12,000 – but I think you can just about get away with somewhere between 500 and 1,000 copies these days, and you make it up on the digital sales.

PM: How is the digital market for Buzzin' Fly – is that the majority now or is it still primarily the vinyl?

BW: Digital has outstripped vinyl sales by, in a lot of cases, three
to one now. If we sell 500 copies of a 12" we'll be selling maybe
15,000 of the lead track off it, another 500 of the B-side, as individual downloads, and that's a good return really, making up for
the money you lose on the manufacturing of only 500 pieces of
vinyl, printing costs and so on. But I think it's important for the
aesthetic of the label, the roots of the label, that we keep making
vinyl, and every now and then we'll put out a big track and we'll
shift 2–3,000 copies of the vinyl and all breathe a sigh of relief
again. It is tough these days.

So even in the field of dance music, which it would seem should be
safe dry ground for the vinyl record, it seems that the 'invisible' format
of the download is outstripping the physical formats – the jukebox of
the hard drive. This made me wonder how the niche market in which
Buzzin' Fly operates differed in its practices and ground rules from
the early indie and mainstream pop fields that Everything but the Girl
worked in.

PM: Have you noticed whether the dance music industry in which
Buzzin' Fly is working employs a different business model to the,
for want of a better term, mainstream rock and pop industry?
BW: Oh yes, traditionally, it's the Wild West . . . it's a sort of
cash-in-hand culture . . . a kid comes up with a great track, he
gets paid a few hundred quid, and never expects to see another
penny. There might be technically speaking a one-sided contract
that he signs, giving him a 50/50 profit share on the track but
often he'd never see that money. Sometimes it's not even cor-
ruption, it's more incompetence, people bite off more than they
can chew, they start their own labels and they don't understand
about accountancy and royalty procedures and when the crunch
comes they have to do a the bookkeeping and that side of things
derails a lot of companies I think. There's some basic small-
business practice that needs to go on to make it work, Certainly
in this day and age . . . Marianne, who's my label manager, has
been with me at Buzzin' Fly since day one. To start with her role
was much more of a traditional label manager, where she would
be involved in the product management of putting a record out,
organising all the printing and the manufacture, making sure
couriers were picking up acetates, all the phone calls side of it,
but now the large proportion of her time is in royalty accounting.
Digital sales these days just come through in so many different

and various streams that you just can't keep on top of it; you'll have sales on Beat Port, iTunes, all the other digital service providers, all with different price points, then you'll be paid funny little penny rates for streaming, through Nokia and Spotify and all these things, and you get your digital statement through and whereas in the old days you might have five line items – 12" sales in the UK, 12" sales for export, Ireland, wherever . . . now you can have up to 6,000 line items on a sheet from your distributor, some of them are for just one cent! Now some poor bookkeeper has to keep track of all that, and that is one of the realities of modern record labels. People often say, oh it's all digital, it's all free, there are no production costs, no distribution costs, how can you charge the same old fashioned royalty rates that labels did when they were dealing with physical product? All that's happened is costs have shifted into a different place. Digital distribution has presented its own set of problems and costs and one of them is accounting – the amount of time that you have to put in for accounting properly for distribution is very, very expensive!

PM: You must need an army of people.

BW: [laughs] That's right, and they're all looking at me!

PM: That leads me on to the next question really: the label started just from you and your interest in and passion for this music which you saw disappearing so decided to do something about getting it heard more widely – how many people are on the team at Buzzin' Fly? What does it take to run a label like this now?

BW: Well we have a small team I suppose: I'm a workaholic, and Marianne works full time for me, we also have someone in the office who does a lot of the in-house press and promotion, also running the webshop, putting together itineraries for our live events, so they cover as Marianne's assistant and also do press and promotion. Then we have a bookkeeper who comes in who works largely from home, and comes in twice a month to make sure the books are all up to scratch, and then we have a small team of interns, often young upcoming DJs or people who just want to get involved in the scene and just come in for a few hours a week for us, helping stuff t-shirts in envelopes for the webshop and so on, trawling Google for weblinks That's the hardcore staff . . . I would love to be able to employ more but sales don't justify it. When we have a bigger project, we take on freelancers, independents, press officer or radio plugger, if it's really big project that we think warrants it.

Watt's detailing of the practical realities of the distinctly unglamor-
ous aspects of running a record label – the bookkeeping, accountancy,
the penny-royalties, the budget balancing – are, as he notes, strangely
unchanged by the absence of great volumes of physical product. Indeed
somewhere they seem to become ever more central to the successful
running of a label. Likewise the financial strictures enforce a more disciplined approach to income and outgoings than has been traditionally
the case in the music industry – this culture of excess has been well
detailed in Dennen (1991), Goodman (1998) and Knopper (2009) for
example. His humorous observation that his employees are 'all looking
at me!' is realistic too – it's not just a matter of sales and returns, commercial success or failure, but rather that people's livelihoods are at
stake. So, given the tight margins and the need to adapt quickly and
nimbly to changes in their market, how to widen the scope of possible
income for the organisation? Dealing in dance music and having a
'name' boss presents an opportunity to Buzzin' Fly by foregrounding
and developing club nights. Ben Watt began DJ'ing before he began
the label so there is an organic link between the two practices; at first
he effectively *was* Buzzin' Fly but subsequently the organisation spread
to accommodate other musicians and Ds under the label's umbrella. I
asked Ben about the role of the DJ set and the club night in how the
organisation works.

> PM: I wonder if we can talk about your DJ sets and so on . . . I'm
> interested in how the label travels . . . if you look at your website,
> it's an impressive itinerary! Australia, Europe, Japan all this year
> [2010] . . . how do you manage that, taking a 'label' rather than a
> musical act on the road – how did that global spread come about,
> and how do you feel about it ?
>
> BW: One of the great advantages of DJ culture is that it has very
> low overheads when you travel. When you put a band on tour,
> immediately you've got four people on the road, four hotel
> rooms, backline, equipment, all that, it's expensive to support
> and you need a very dedicated bunch of kids doing it. The beauty
> with DJ'ing is you get the last flight out of Heathrow on a Friday
> night, one overnight bag and a bag of records which you can
> carry on as hand luggage, they turn up in a European city, they're
> picked up by the promoter, dropped off at the hotel, picked up
> an hour later, taken to the club, and play a venue from 400 up
> to 2,000 people and get paid what a band would get paid. That's
> the basic economics of it – so that's how you can afford to take a
> label brand on the road so easily. That's really how we do it . . .

we try to make sure that the parties we throw involve at least one key DJ or producer who has been involved in the label at one level to represent us, and then we'll strike a deal with the local promoter, so that all the posters and flyers have to be graphically designed to fit the label and so on – in fact we will often provide the artwork as part of the deal.

In the bigger venues we'll go to the lengths of providing 35 mm slides, to decorate the venue in some way, so you try to present the vibe of the label and provide the DJs to play music that suits the aesthetic and ethos of the label. That's how we do it and because of that you can be in various cities on one weekend, if you get it right, with me playing in Australia and Charles Webster playing in Greece, Chris Woodford playing in Istanbul . . . the Holy Grail for me is being able to create these Buzzin' Fly parties where I don't have to play myself! [laughs] This has been the big struggle because everyone wants a Buzzin' Fly party with me playing. So in the face of struggling record sales we've put a lot of effort in the past twelve months into upping our event side, and it's now accounting for over 30 per cent of the label's income, and we need that extra injection of capital to keep the label afloat.

PM: Apart from anything else it gets the music heard and people pass it on . . .

BW: Definitely, it creates a little buzz in the city where you're playing, local DJs talk to each other . . . it does work I think.

This idea of a global presence, where Buzzin' Fly can run club nights simultaneously on different continents is an impressive indicator of how far the label has come and also, as Watt mentions, one of the advantages of 'DJ culture'. It both relies upon and can alter the meaning of the records they play. In some ways it is a happy by-product of technology not unlike that offered by recorded music itself – a song and a singer can be 'present' in millions of homes, clubs or collections simultaneously, even after they have passed over; thanks to the mediations of recording my children know who Elvis and Michael Jackson were and can listen to them as freely as I ever could when I was at school. I asked him about a specific evening on his 2010 tour list.

PM: You did a set in Prague not long ago . . . how did that work?

BW: Well almost exactly as I described it before – different DJs have different styles, some love the weekend experience and are complete party animals, they might get an earlier flight out, do a bit of sightseeing, start drinking early, have a laugh, go on to an after-hours after their own set, early hours of the morning, stay over another day, being thrilled that they're being paid for doing what they love. [*PM*: Behave like the traditional rock musician on tour, I suppose.] Exactly, but as for me these days I tend to be a lot more business like about it, you know I've got a family, I've got record labels to run, radio shows to make, so I prefer to be more like a Navy Seal, you know, get in under the cover of darkness, blow up the harbour and get out again! So I'll get as late a flight as I can, don't expect dinner, I'll sort myself out with food, arrive quite late, go for a drink with the promoter, do the gig, go back to the hotel then I'll get a flight home shortly after lunch the next day. That was the Prague schedule, to a T.

The Buzzin' Fly identity has been carefully built to be not simply a pseudonym for Ben Watt; rather it stands for a kind of quality of experience, a signifier of a certain set of musical and aesthetic values and criteria, driven by but not wholly synonymous with those of the label's founder. That spreading of the identity of the label extends into broadcast media too, via the Buzzin' Fly radio show, a monthly two-hour package which showcases some of the label's catalogue, though not exclusively, alongside a very wide range of music. Indeed it is the show's eclecticism which is a key part of its appeal – we examine a single episode later.

> *PM*:   I'm interested in the radio show – could I just ask you about how you set that up, how it works and what you think the function of that is?
>
> *BW*:   Sure – historically there are lots of examples of DJs who had successful radio shows – top of the tree probably Pete Tong, on Kiss Jon Digweed, at a more eclectic level people like Rob Da Bank and Gilles Peterson, they've all got their own place in the radio world . . . I didn't really have any plans for a radio show and then Galaxy approached me, three or four years ago, asked whether I'd be interested in doing a show based around the label and my taste and I jumped at the chance, thought it would be fun. I basically make the show at home, either do it in my home studio or on my laptop when I'm travelling, all I need is a microphone, and when it's finished I send it to the station that's going to broadcast it in good time and they add any additional 'stings' and 'ident's all over it that they want so it sounds like it's

going out on their station. I did two years on Galaxy, and then Kiss picked it up and it was on Kiss until January this year (2010), but they've now just squeezed their specialist programming and didn't want Buzzin' Fly for this year, but I've kept the show going . . . we did a bit of market research when Kiss dropped the show and it transpired that Kiss were responsible for only about 6 per cent of the total listenership anyway and syndications now on stations around the world and the webstream itself accounts for the vast proportion of the people who are listening to it. But there are some nice quirky anomalies, for example I didn't know until quite recently that the show goes out on drivetime in Istanbul, on a Friday night! Ever since I found out about this I just imagine these people driving home from work, it's around 7 it goes out I think, Friday night on their local dance station, I just think that's wonderful, regardless of whether it's good for Buzzin' Fly or not.

PM: I like the idea of the radio show . . . part of the 360 degree thing.

BW: Exactly – you can get inside it and walk around a bit, some evidence of reality. Now that I've been released from the demands of Kiss, I've loosened up the content a bit, and you'll find more of the kind of stuff you might find on the other label I run, Strange Feeling. A bit more indie I suppose, I'm quite pleased I'm able to do that, Kiss had slightly stronger restrictions on what they wanted from me. Which was fair enough, they have that urban dance remit.

PM: You've also done some shows for the BBC's recently saved 6 Music – how did that come about?

BW: 6 Music offered me a one-off two-hour show on their 6Mix show in June 2010 as they liked my show and felt I would chime with and appeal to the 6 Music listeners. It went well, so when they were looking for new rotating residents in the autumn they came back. I have been booked for six more shows over twelve months rotating with Errol Alkan, Derrick May and others.

The invitation to make shows for the BBC says much about the slowly building success of the Buzzin' Fly imprint, and it is notable that the feel of the show did not change appreciably in this more mainstream broadcasting environment. The remit of the radio show, released from the 'urban dance' strictures required by Kiss FM, has been able to develop and wander more freely across the range of styles that the mother label touches upon and this willingness to move away from the expected models of content and delivery is also connected to the developing sense of Buzzin' Fly as more than a 'dance music' label.

Regardless of the quality of the music or the aesthetic that surrounds it, if the product isn't available to buy then financial ruin awaits any label, independent or not. So how does Buzzin' Fly ensure that the music gets into the right commercial outlets?

> *PM*:   How difficult – or easy – was it to get Buzzin' Fly product into the right places to get it heard, played and sold?
>
> *BW*:   In the end you're nothing if the content isn't strong enough, especially in dance music. I always believe that the dance floor never lies – you can't make a hit club track out of a bad club track. It either works on the dance floor or it doesn't. Whatever the DJ is doing, if the audience doesn't agree with them, you're nowhere. I don't think Buzzin' Fly would have survived if the records we put out hadn't been popular at some level, among other DJs and on other dance floors. So that is the first thing. People have to like it, or no amount of pushing and plugging is going to help. There are constant examples of tiny labels these days bubbling up and breaking through this saturated market with three or four really great tracks, and suddenly you think 'what's that little label from Oslo that's on its fifth release now, I like the first three . . .' It's like the old days Peter! [Laughs] If there's three or four great tracks from one label, it breaks through . . . it requires good production, from the artist in the first place, good A & R-ing at the record label level, the tracks have to be well-mastered to sound great on the dance floor – you're half way there if you get that stuff right. Geoff Travis at Rough Trade always used to say, life on independent record labels is content driven; if that's not right, all the other padding isn't going to help, it's not going to go anywhere. There's that side of it – also there was a bit of leverage because of my relative fame, but you could also look at that and see that it might have been damaging in some way, I had quite a lot of stuff to break through as well . . . a bit of suspicion, here was somebody from essentially the pop mainstream, muscling in on the underground, trying to tell us how to do it, so there was quite a bit of that in the early days, from some areas, but you just press on.

So bearing in mind Geoff Travis's observation about life on an independent label being 'content driven' it's worth reflecting on how that might impact upon the creativity as well as the business side of things for a label like Buzzin' Fly – after all, Ben Watt is a creative person by nature, a musician, writer and producer, and has learned about business as he has gone along. He hints at this point at which business and commerce meet in his reflection upon the need to ensure a track be well mastered so it sounds good and full and crisp through a club sound system – in order to recognise this sound as the 'right' one requires a great 'ear' as well as some business acumen as to what has the potential to sell well. Watt's natural inclination to move with deft ease between apparently diverse musical styles also serves him well, in that he sees feelingly the connections as well as the distinctions between genres – this will have been part of his being able to weather the criticisms of his early DJ'ing and production of electronic dance music. Yet dance music as a 'scene' always seemed less tribal than the hardline distinctions practised in the fields of rock and pop, and extending into subcultural affiliations as scrutinised by everyone from Cohen (1966) via Hebdige (1979) to Muggleton (2000). I asked about this idea.

PM: Maybe it's a misapprehension, but the dance scene always seems more democratic than rock and pop . . . people are listening to what's there rather than saying 'it's okay but I can't like it because of x, y and z . . .'

BW: Well that's true, I think . . . one of the things I love about dance music is that it is ultimately a community experience . . . the music comes alive in that joint relationship between the DJ and the people in the club. Late at night when your defences are down a little bit, you're under the influence of alcohol or drugs, you enter this slightly looser world, where no one is really in charge . . . the music really is the most important thing. That's what I love about it . . . it's quite ritualistic..

PM: It's experienced collectively . . . there's a mood in the room.

BW: Yeah, that's right, if a track bubbles up and starts to dominate the atmosphere . . . I might have played it at the 'right time' but it's the music that has the power . . . I love that slightly shamanistic, ritualistic thing, especially having been in the pop mainstream for so long, which is often about everyone sitting facing the stage, often in reverential silence, as was frequently the case with Everything But The Girl, and that can be very claustrophobic. So going into clubs is a kind of freedom. Even now, five years into Buzzin' Fly, DJs and record people know the label, but when I walk into a club I'd say 85 per cent of the people still don't really know who I am. You are just the guy in the booth who has

to rock the floor, and I kind of like that 'head in the lions mouth'
thing.

PM: You've got to make something happen . . .

BW: Yes, you have, you're not a star, you've just got to play the
records in the right order. [*PM*: The alchemic formula.] Yes, and
I really like that about it.

Watt identifies some interesting points about differences between
audiences and also the prescribed codes of behaviour for those audiences, be they in the concert hall or the club. They may of course be
the same individuals – any one person may go to a folk club, a classical recital and a Buzzin' Fly night in the same week and enjoy them
equally – but different rules guide their conduct and responses in each
context. Hence his observation of the shamanistic, ritualistic element
to the club atmosphere is highlighting both what can and cannot be
undertaken in such an environment – these are the rules, even if it feels
like an absence of rules. What is key, and indeed common, to any of
our imagined contexts is that the music is placed at the centre of the
ritual and all activity is guided by and organised around that power –
we move and are moved by it accordingly. So if it is not simply a case
of cranking out a series of repetitive beats, I wondered what it was he
listened for in a Buzzin' Fly track:

PM: What would you say is characteristic of a Buzzin' Fly record?
Is there a 'sound' that marks a track out as a Buzzin' Fly track?
I hear an intriguing mix of the contemporary . . . percussively
I mean, it's determinedly rhythmic in that way, but there's a
gospel-soul thing that keeps breaking through too . . . is that fair?

BW: It's pathos, isn't it? That undercurrent of pathos, that I've
tried to find in everything I've ever done . . . people use words
in reviews of Buzzin' Fly releases, like emotive or emotional or
deep, and I think what they're alluding to is that I do choose
music, apart from as you say the percussive drive of the track,
that has an element of the blues, has that element of pathos in
it, in the chord changes, it's in the melodies I'm attracted to,
because for me that is the ultimate goal, to inject music with
enough energy to make you want to get up out of your seat, but
also to move you in your spirit and get under your skin. That's
the driving force behind the kind of music we put out.

When I was conducting this interview, one of the very last words I
would have guessed he would answer this question with would have

been 'pathos'. Yet as noted earlier, one thing which binds together the disparate elements of the Everything but the Girl catalogue is the line of continuity represented by the emotional human voice alongside the strictly rhythmic dimension. In reaching for this term he joins together all the phases of his substantial body of work before and after the setting up of the label as a line of connective continuity, drawing together musical styles and the practical tasks (which are also artistic and aesthetic tests) of writing, assembling and marketing that music in the way that serves it to its best advantage. The pathos of a tune like 'Lone Cat' is clearly of a different cast to that of his early tunes like 'North Marine Drive' or 'Easy as Sin', but by identifying this common thread we see how what drives a successful record label and the basic creative impulse need not be contradictory forces. The business sense learned along the way colludes with the intuitive knowledge of what makes for a moving and effective piece of music, regardless of the genre, and the signs are strong that this may be the right blend which enables Buzzin' Fly not only to survive but to thrive in a newly configured marketplace.

Case study II: Pure Records

Kate Rusby is probably the most successful artist to emerge from the British folk scene in the last twenty years. Mystifyingly, given her popularity and musical gift, her work has been overlooked in studies and histories of the field such as Brocken (2003), Sweers (2005) and Young (2010). This may in some way be due to the way she has managed to transcend the usual categories and genre barriers which seem to divide musical styles from each other in the marketplace. So while you'll certainly find her albums filed in the 'Folk' browser at the music store, her appeal has spread far beyond the limits of that particular constituency. She has been nominated for the Mercury Prize, won a fistful of folk awards from various sources and made albums with her friend Kathryn Roberts and as a member of renowned folk group the Poozies alongside Karen Tweed. Since releasing her first solo album *Hourglass* in 1995, she has steadily climbed to a position where she is arguably the best known and most recognisable figure in English folk song, is genuinely and widely popular and is blessed with a very loyal audience. She has so far issued nine solo albums and one DVD, *Live From Leeds*, and a second Christmas album, *While Mortals Sleep*, is scheduled for November 2011. To her credit she has not recorded albums of covers or Beatles tunes in an effort to crossover into the pop market, sticking instead to the same basic formula – every couple of years, an album of a dozen or so tunes, usually a mix of traditional songs and her own compositions, although 2010's *Make The Light* broke the mould somewhat in being entirely self-penned. Often it is difficult to distinguish her originals from the traditional material, so deeply has she absorbed the traditions of the style and so deft and intuitive is her use and understanding of those traditions.

For our purposes, what makes this success all the more intriguing is that it has been achieved without her being signed to a major record label or, indeed, one of the many robust independents that have dominated the British folk scene for many years such as Topic, Cooking Vinyl or Greentrax. Instead, since day one, Kate Rusby's music has been issued on the family's own label, Pure. This is a situation almost without precedent in the British music scene. Even within the independent sector, where many acts have their own labels, the usual case is that sales are at a modest and easily manageable level, or that there might be one or two 'breakout' hits on such a label and the profits arising from any such success would be ploughed back into the label so that it might expand. A good example of this would be the unlikely, John Peel-sponsored success of 1980s Birkenhead group Half Man Half Biscuit, whose album *Back in the DHSS* and subsequent singles allowed Probe Records, which was run out of the city's premier independent record shop of the same name, to revise their ambitions and sign a slew of other local acts. None of these, however, made any commercial impression. Furthermore, once a certain level of commercial success is reached, the label 'imprint' may be sold to a major and becomes part of a larger organisation, granting access to promotional and distribution 'muscle' denied to the smaller independent set-up. In the process the value and meaning of independence can be easily dispersed, dissolved or simply disappear, and the label name becomes merely a vanity imprint. Major independents, if that is not a contradiction in terms, are often obliged to behave like mainstream major labels in order to survive – this may well be seen via changed business models, in the budgets for promotional videos/campaigns and so on, or via changed relationships with acts and/or independent record retailers. Sometimes it may be that the 'family silver' has to be sold, as in the case of Rough Trade selling the Smiths catalogue to Sony in the early 1990s, which began the process of repackaging and 'Best Ofs' that still continue. This, as documented by Taylor (2010), was necessary to save the Rough Trade organisation as a whole from financial ruin.

What marks Pure out as special and interesting for us is the way it has both managed great commercial success and kept absolutely true to its original business model; it is a true independent label which has the kind of turnover which many a major in this difficult period for the music industry would cherish. It is successful in every possible sense and delivers very high-quality product both via the studio and on tour yet it is effectively still run as it was back in 1995, as a well-managed business but also as a kind of labour of love, a contemporary cottage industry. A particular virtue of Pure is that it also has a strong catalogue of recordings aside from the Kate Rusby albums – for example, the label has issued albums by playwright and family friend Willy Russell, the soundtrack to Billy Connolly's TV series about his trip to New Zealand, and highly regarded solo works by Maggie Boyle, John McCusker, Roddy Woomble and Damien O'Kane, all of which received the same standards of presentation afforded to Kate Rusby's output. Records as remarkable as Kris Drever's *Black Water* have been recorded at Pure's in-house studio, too. The Rusby family run the whole operation, with Kate's father Steve being her manager, her mother Ann being in charge of the budget and the bookkeeping, sister Emma in charge of promotion, PR and everything in-between, and brother Joe as producer in the on-site Pure recording studio in South Yorkshire and taking very capable care of in-concert sound on the road. So the family is uniquely skilled and well placed to all contribute something both distinctive and important to the project. I asked Ann, Emma and Steve Rusby how this remarkable state of independence came to be.

AR: Well, right back in the beginning we'd tried to get something together when Kate had decided this was what she wanted to do, and record companies said 'come back when she's better known' . . . so we sat down, Steve had finished in Leeds [where Steve Rusby worked at the Leeds College of Music] and I'd packed in teaching, and said, well, let's do it ourselves.

SR: We talked to the right people at the right time . . . but when Kate and Kathryn [Roberts] started to become popular in the folk clubs the act started getting squashed down a bit, yet people were coming to see them, rather than the usual thing in the folk club – which is the fantastic thing about them – where everyone wants to join in. So everyone wants to sing to a full room, but it was Kate and Kathryn's crowd, so that made it more complicated . . . people who didn't usually frequent the folk clubs were coming along wanting to see the girls and at 11 o'clock they're still waiting for them to come on . . . so eventually I had to contract it that their spot would begin no later than quarter past ten.

It became clear that what people wanted to do was come to a nice venue, listen to what they wanted to listen to, and go. The folk clubs ran according to a different set of rules and expectations to that.

Ann Rusby's comment 'Well, let's do it ourselves' makes the complex task seem straightforward and this clear-sightedness, based on watchful experience, is perhaps part of the root of Pure's successful business model. So from the outset there was clearly something which set both the music and the business models employed to showcase it to its best advantage, apart from the normal run of things – an act that took its place in the running order of the folk club, a system ideologically weighted against showbusiness conventions of 'star billing', yet which drew in a crowd specifically to see them – in other words a crowd behaving like an audience at a much bigger venue or in another musical genre altogether. As Steve Rusby notes, the folk club circuit, for all its very many virtues, is not necessarily set up to work this way. His astute management of his daughter's career is shown to have been at work since the start – 'I had to contract it that their spot would begin no later than a quarter past ten'.

The traditional route for a new act who has a record to promote is to move from the small spots at the local club to a support slot on a tour with an act which is related to their own style and tone; wildly mismatched support/main act combinations are rare. For Kate Rusby having no agent or promoter to please, such dues-paying was not strictly necessary, and those she did were hardly at the bottom in terms of the folk hierarchy: 'She hardly ever did supports actually . . . she did one for Billy Bragg, and one for Richard Thompson for about a week.' Furthermore, Pure decided not to hire support acts once she made the step up to the bigger venues; again, this is a radical step for a new act and one designed not to compromise the direct idea of presentation and promotion that Pure sought to employ.

> SR: We've never really had supports. When she moved into the arts centres, and onto a more professional basis, we decided on no support, and two 45-minute spots . . . and that's what we still do now . . .
>
> ER: An agent would have a stable of acts they needed to deal with too . . . Kate went straight from folk clubs, with Kathryn, to the bigger venues, there was just them, no other up-and-coming acts that an agent might present and promote, there was just her, so we weren't pushing anybody else.

The focus of the operation was not the instigation of a stable of acts, as it might be for even the smallest independent label, the number of acts being able to increase the chances of some kind of breakthrough propping up the operation – we recall the example of Half Man Half Biscuit and Liverpool's Probe Records. Instead, the focus was the promotion and consolidation of the success of Kate Rusby's work. Thus from the off, Pure stood outside the usual guidelines of a traditional independent record label in that it focused on one act alone, had its own studio, its own PA and organised and promoted its own tours. The *Kate Rusby and Kathryn Roberts* album, issued in 1995 by Pure, was a document of their set from the folk clubs and bore a sleeve note that looked to the future and the past in equal measure, and reads like both a manifesto and a valedictory message.

> Although this is our debut recording, this album has been a long time in the making – almost 20 years! It contains childhood memories which we hope to share with other people, as they have shared with us. For the uninitiated, the traditional music scene has a respect and love for people, as well as the music, which is unrivalled anywhere else. We feel privileged to have been nurtured in it and proud to say that these are our roots.

In this little note, candid and purposeful, is a grateful acknowledgement of the past and the sense of continuity that singing these songs and passing them along brings; equally present is the sense that they are moving on from the roots too, making something new from the schooling they have received. That double sense of purpose is a source of great strength, placing Rusby and Roberts in a chain of tradition which reaches back while moving forward. This kind of refreshed stream of tradition informed the way the new Pure organisation set about its business, too. The LP remains the only Kate Rusby album to have not have been recorded at Pure's in-house studio, being recorded in Temple Studios in Edinburgh under the production of John McCusker. Its success was the first stone in the building of the Pure organisation beyond a label name. Even before it was issued, however, the landscape had changed and things began to move quickly, as Ann Rusby recalled:

> *AR*: By the time the Kate and Kathryn album came out, things had happened with a group of boys from Exeter, the Lakemans, who were instrumental musicians in the main, and they wanted singers in their act. They asked Kate if she'd join and she said 'I'm with Kathryn' so they said bring her as well! So they had a

five-piece, called Equation, who were spotted by Geoff Travis at Rough Trade who wanted to sign them for Blanco y Negro. He was excited by the group and wanted them in his stable. So Kate rang us up from Exeter and said 'this man is coming from London to talk to us . . . I don't want to be part of it, although everyone else wants to'. They were talking about clothes and hair and so on, being moulded, and Kate didn't want any part of it. But Kathryn and the boys did, they wanted to go that way, so the girls split and by the time the Kate and Kathryn album came out, Kathryn was on her way.

This is an intriguing story and one which reveals much about Kate Rusby's approach to both the creative side of music making and to machinations of the music industry at large. 'The Lakemans' were Seth, Sam and Sean Lakeman, subsequently all successful folk musicians. I asked Steve Rusby why Kate might have turned down the chance of signing to a 'major independent' like Blanco y Negro, as part of Equation – after all, it would have been with the personal imprimatur of Geoff Travis, head of the mother of all UK indie labels, Rough Trade.

> *PM*: Why did Kate not want to be involved in a project like that, do you think?
>
> *SR*: Because she wanted to plough her own furrow . . . before all this we'd had long discussions about how to find a record label . . . Topic were interested, The Battlefield Band's label Temple, various people were interested, we could have done that . . . but Kate knows the business and didn't want to do that . . . and our record was going good! So when someone comes along with a five record deal and a million pounds, we weren't swayed because we knew what that meant! So Kate left the Equation project, and did a bit of solo work, and then she was asked to join the Poozies when their singer was off having a baby . . . that was good for her, she got about Europe a lot more . . . they were already established touring Germany and Denmark and so on, so she already had her solo career started, but had the Poozies as well at that time.

The folk ethos of simply playing in a collective spirit rather than focusing on the competitive aspect more familiar from pop and rock marketplace is in evidence here as Kate Rusby's own career and that of the Poozies overlapped happily for a spell. Furthermore we discover that the Rusbys' first thought was not the setting up of their own organisation, rather indeed that they'd considered all the other, obvious options and decided that they were not what they wanted. The Battlefield Band's interest became personal when Kate Rusby eventually married their fiddle player John McCusker, while Topic is the oldest independent folk label in the UK, having been set up in 1939 as an offshoot of the Worker's Music Association. It has been home to virtually all the key figures of British folk music – Ewan MacColl, A. L. Lloyd, the Waterson and Carthy families and Kate Rusby's own musical inspiration, Nic Jones. So to turn down the opportunity to join that roster must have been quite a decision. I wondered how and why the decision was made when it was and how it was:

> SR: Because we had the label going, and Kate's album [*Hourglass*] was going like a steamtrain . . . distributors were all keen to do deals directly with us, she was playing bigger venues and she didn't have the time to contribute as much as she wanted to the Poozies so eventually she told them she'd be leaving at the end of the year. The sales of *Hourglass* were maybe 100,000, which isn't enormous, but all the money has come in to the record company and been administered and distributed by us . . . in terms of folk the sales were just phenomenal, because usually you're looking at an artist selling 1,000, and shifting 5,000 is very good! So our figures were mighty unusual!

Steve Rusby is quite right – sales of 100,000 for an independent label is indeed exceptional, in any genre, but for folk it is quite unheard of. Yet the quality of the music cannot make this happen on its own – many great recordings and recording artists never get near such figures. Pure was deft in making sure the music was heard by the right people and that it was promoted in the right way:

> ER: We did the advertising and the mailing list, so people could go and look for us, but word of mouth was very strong too. Then it was Bryan Ledgard, at his Ledgard Jepson design company, where I used to work, who helped us with the design side of things, he made sure we had good posters, good images, good sleeves. All that side of it was very important too.
>
> SR: And when the money came in, because we were the record company, we could decide what we wanted to do with it! So we ploughed it back in, made sure the covers were good, the posters

were good, all that . . . we can decide what to spend, when we've
spent enough, so it's about being in control of the situation and
our own work . . . it's transparent the way we work . . . there's this
amount of money available, do we want to spend some more?
So an act that is signed to a company sells a thousand and says
'where's our money', and the company says 'it cost more than
that to advertise it!' We're free of all that.

Here we find the real meaning of independence within the music marketplace. Steve Rusby's appraisal of the company's position posits a
brand new model for the recording, promoting and selling of popular
music which seems entirely relaxed in its freedoms from the constraints of traditional music business models, instead simply seeing
what needs to be done and being able to do it. There is something
appropriately 'folk' about this plainness but, in terms of the music
industry, it is what makes Pure so revolutionary yet also so successful. Emma's observation about the actual practical tasks of packaging
and managing the public image of the artist show too that while Pure
is a family affair they are quite open to contributions from without,
should the task fall outside their own experience, technical expertise or
natural capacities. It is indeed notable that high production values are
what marks out the early Kate Rusby album sleeves and poster designs
from the norm – in independent folk, certainly, and the wider indie
sector as a whole. Even a plain portrait like that featured on the cover
of *Hourglass* is framed by a neat checkerboard design which echoes
the pattern on Rusby's clothing in the shot. Similarly, her second
album *Sleepless* has a complex collage design more familiar from rock,
pop or even jazz sleeve design, while subsequent Kate Rusby albums
like *Underneath the Stars* and, especially, *Little Lights* catch her in rich
colour on a sumptuous and sensual lightscape. But, of course, there
is a reason why indie labels are associated with more basic packaging
techniques – the cost of lavish photography and rich colour images
may well be prohibitive. This is something which, with the early
success of Kate Rusby's commercial releases and live performances,
Pure was better placed than some to deal with, but costs were still
something of which they were mindful:

> *ER*:   It's knowing how much it all costs . . . you can spend endless
> amounts on ads and CD singles and so on but it all costs . . .
> everything you do is paid for, the record shop racking is paid for,
> all by discount or trading off but you have to make a decision
> about what you're going to spend for the return you're going to

get to make sure they're in the shops. It can be a struggle to keep them in stock.

SR: Part of the difficulty is that Kate is put in the 'Folk' box, and the currency of folk is low as far as the mainstream shops are concerned.

AR: The 'Folk' thing always keeps them on their guard, even when they know how well Kate's albums sell.

The lifetime of Pure is almost a casebook in itself of how the selling and marketing of music has changed; Steve Rusby recalled that both the Rusby/Roberts and *Hourglass* albums were commercially issued on cassette tape, a format which, in mainstream marketing terms, is now long redundant. Likewise, Emma observed that the formats in which they routinely trade now did not even exist when Pure began and the traditional outlets – the record shops – are in a serious if not terminal decline: 'There's only HMV on the high street now – when we began there were three or four names.' This has forced the hand of an operation like Pure into the digital realm – either via online retail of physical product (old-fashioned mail order by any other name) or via downloads.

Pure was quite an 'early adopter' of online retailing via their own website – initially via physical product and moving into downloads later. The first release to be made available first and primarily via download from Pure's website was her 2008 cover of Sandy Denny's 'Who Knows Where the Time Goes', originally recorded for the BBC series *Jam and Jerusalem*. I asked about the relative role the download plays in the sales of the Pure catalogue:

SR: For Kate's last album [then *Sweet Bells*] I'd say we've sold 80 per cent on the Internet, most of the rest at shows and then some in the shops.

PM: Eighty per cent as downloads?

SR: No, as CDs from our site and Amazon.

AR: We tended to ignore the digital for a while, when iTunes and Amazon were all taking off.

SR: Well, we didn't ignore it so much . . . we put up some downloads on Kate's website fairly early on, so from the early days you've been able to download Kate's product that way, song by song if you like. But then iTunes got so big you can't ignore it. We've never licensed the digital rights to anybody; it's all done worldwide by us.

ER: They didn't really exist to begin with . . . when the first albums went over there [the US], digital rights weren't an issue.

SR: But they came into later contracts with our American licensee, so we said no . . . we administer them from here. So now
Amazon and Play now amount to about 80 per cent of sales.

ER: This is the way it's going. My son never goes near a record
shop. He downloads. That's it.

So although they were at first tentative in their connections with the
major commercial digital providers Pure soon saw this as the way
forward for marketing and sales, with the important caveat that, as
with the physical product, they remained firmly in control of the
rights. This ability to respond to the new conditions in such a way that
is consistent with their existing business model is what marks Pure out
as something quite remarkable in the marketplace, be that digital or
otherwise. The relatively modest size of the organisation enables these
decisions to be made with this kind of internal coherence, even when
the sales figures involved are more familiar from the balance sheets of
much bigger and more corporately arranged businesses.

The appeal of the product and the continued demand for it is fully
grounded in the music; in order to keep the contact up with the audience, it is important that the act is active in the concert hall. Kate
Rusby tends to tour most comprehensively in the spring and late
autumn, and since the issue of her Christmas album she has taken to
playing a short run of shows in December at which the seasonal music
is showcased. Great store is placed upon this live connection between
Rusby and her audience and her shows are notable for the folk-club
warmth of the atmosphere – she is known for her good-humoured
monologues between songs and for occasionally gently poking fun at
the more morose aspects of the English folk song. This never intrudes
upon the performances, however, which are always perfectly focused.
This balance is quite distinctive and she treads this fine line with
almost complete ease. But, I wondered, how is the live side of the business managed? It's one thing to have an in-house studio, drive your
own publicity materials and find a business model for marketing and
sales, but playing live shows inevitably means that you will encounter
other ways of working, which may not be set up for dealing with an
organisation that does not necessarily follow the normal music business rules. This requires a kind of reality check – at what stage does the
business and the art intersect?

ER: Once you get into it on a professional level, I don't think
people just do it for fun any more . . . you do it because you love
it to begin with, but then the professional side of it has to come

in to how you work . . . making a living, established rates for live musicians, for recording sessions . . . there's a fair amount of money to be paid but people still do favours. Kate will say 'how much can we afford on that' and that's fine, we work something out, so we are able to pay musicians what they should be paid. The business works well that way . . . .the chaos tends be amongst us, so that we'll always say 'we'll never do it this way again', and announce a release date in what seems plenty of time and then end up racing to meet the date! It always happens that way.

PM: Does the sort of success you've had made it easier or harder to keep that independence?

SR: I think it frees you up, the more successful you become, and although we're the record company for Kate, we're also the agency and management, so there are tiers to all this, levels which have been stripped out of it all. Let's just think about the record company's link to the gig. Normally the artists and record company would talk and arrange the best time to tour, then management would see an agent, who would elect promoters in that area – the geographical area as well as genre of music – so you've already got management, agent, promoter taking a chunk out of it. The management might be concerned about the record, if they have a share in it or they might not, and the other guys don't care about the record at all. So you come to the gig, where you're going to sell it, and there's merchandise and established criteria related to the selling of it, which is usually around 25 per cent, the venue will want that for you selling your product. That's in your contract. So because I set the gigs up, I've always set Kate's gigs up, from when we started in the folk clubs, dealing with the bookers, so I got used to doing it. Consequently we fix our own rates and fees, and the bookers know us, because we deal with them personally. Later we'd meet the established agents, and a few years later, once we were under way and got it cracked, they come to us saying 'can we represent Kate?' You must be joking! Hand it over? I don't think so!

So we're interested in selling records – the first thing we do is a deal, we talk about merchandise. We're bringing this gig in, it's going to sell out, we'll fill your bars up for you, we're going to carry it in, we're going to sell it . . . so you get rid of the merchandise fee – sometimes 25 per cent! – or it gets down to a tolerable percentage, or a facility fee for a table . . . we'll pay you £50. We've had incredible battles over the years about it, but that is a significant thing, about the record company linking in with the rest of it.

The spirit of the independent flares up here in Steve Rusby's appraisal of how they negotiate with established venues and agencies. This is not to say that relationships between Pure and the venues are strained – far from it. Indeed, this can be seen by the great number of return bookings Kate Rusby receives. There is a circuit of venues at which she has to some degree found her level, and aside from occasional forays into less traditional theatres, such as 2009's visit to O2 in London, her tours tend to stick to these locations. For example her 2010 'Christmas' tour took in London, Gateshead, Harrogate, Whitby, Cardiff, Sheffield, Newton in Powys and Nottingham. This is as good as mix of the traditional folk music friendly small theatre/art centre circuit and the mainstream bigger venue as you'd care to find. This mix characterises her schedules, managing to keep her long-standing audience connected (Sheffield, Harrogate) while also reaching out to less-well visited areas, such as Newton in Powys and Whitby. The big shows in London, Gateshead and Cardiff are all evidence of her great commercial appeal – these are big venues and take some selling out, yet Kate Rusby shows routinely do sell out, whatever the venue.

> *ER*:   When we are on tour, everybody conducts themselves well, they leave things tidy, they're polite to people, and that all makes a difference . . .
> *PM*:   So you deal with the venues directly?
> *ER*:   Directly, yes. So if we want to play in York, we book the theatre, she goes and plays it. There's no promoter . . . because the groundwork's done. We got rid of the agents taking a cut . . .
> *ER*:   As for the record company paying to fund the artist on tour, we've always treated it as two quite separate things; the record does what the record does, and we pay for advertising and posters and the rest, while the gigs pay for themselves. If you're going on tour, you've got 'X' amount of money, what are you going to do with it?
> *SR*:   We've heard of people who go on tour, sell well yet come out with a £50,000 debt . . .

Clearly experience and observation has taught Pure what to do as well as what not to do. The division of the recording and the live ventures into distinct, self-funding activities has reaped rewards, and also insulated each from the vagaries of the other – for example, when Pure's distributor Pinnacle collapsed in December 2008 they were able to manage their own distribution until they found another home. The initial release of *Sweet Bells* in that same month was hit by Pinnacle's demise and so in the following December 2009 they chose to reissue the album in a new cover; again we see here how the scale of the operation enables Pure to pick a pathway through the media landscape, adapting quickly to changed conditions. The live shows, however, help the records of course – they provide publicity and the opportunity for high-volume sales. This is good news for Pure – and also Kate Rusby's audience – as while the high street retail price on Pure product is £14.99, the albums are available at the shows for usually £10–£12. This income is, again, kept within the operation as a whole as they have rarely if ever taken a support act on the road with them (*ER:* 'We learned fast that you don't take more musicians than you can pay, feed or afford to look after . . . take a support on tour and you have to pay them, accommodate them, transport them') and the typical Rusby show is indeed without support. Now, as Steve Rusby says, 'What we've learned being out on tour with loads of people, is that the merchandise sells in the break' but the selling isn't the only logic at work here.

SR: So we come back to the way we organise ourselves. Kate will probably do an hour each side now, with a 20-minute interval . . . people have time to get home and maybe even have a pint before they clock off, and that works fine for us.

Booking themselves into a network of venues usually geared up for dealing with agencies and corporate promoters can lead to difficulties, however, of scale and of timing, especially as planning for a December tour approaches. We spoke about this:

SR: As for the Christmas shows, we think great, big show, get the brass band boys in . . . what happens? Most of the venues have pantos in . . . so you have to be very careful! But we book up to a year in advance sometimes, depending on where and when. You have to.

ER: Yes you might have Sunday afternoon from 2 o'clock onwards only, that might be the only slot so you have to be in and out very quick sometimes; the larger gigs have to be planned so far ahead . . . for example, the Sage at Gateshead or the Royal Festival Hall [both booked for the December 2010 run of shows], so part of what I do is when the itinerary is worked out,

I talk to the venue and get the publicity sorted out, I'll say OK give me a press list, and I'll send out to local press in the area . . . a little bit of a promoter job. This is the same as when she was playing smaller gigs, you still need to get the word out . . . 'can you give us a mention, an interview? Fantastic!' And the monthlies are working so far ahead you have do it . . . and it's easier now of course because people know us now . . . but that's fifteen years on from saying 'would you please?' The venues have publicity machines as well but they're dealing with everybody. So I find it easier to deal with the venues individually rather than have a list of people we ask to do it for us. We take as little paid advertising as we possibly can by chasing the editorial stuff.

PM: That's right, I rarely see posters advertising tours or new releases.

ER: Well, there are times we do take the national advertising when there's a lot going on but by and large we try and get away with as little as possible. Instead we use the Internet, the mailing list, word of mouth . . .

So here we see how the promotional brief takes in both the established routes of the magazines and the press in tandem, typical of the name act, and the direct approach to the venues which is usually associated with the very early stages of an act's professional career. The coexistence of these two modes of promotion and arrangement mark out Pure's policy as most unusual. In Emma's final trio of methods, we move from the newest of media ('Internet') right back to the very oldest ('word of mouth') and in the process we see how they are connected – both are means to an end, that of direct communication.

The 360 degree nature of the operation becomes plain; there is a lot for Pure to do and to exert control over yet they do it with ease and with good humour, adapting where they can and allowing new communication media to take up some of the strain, leaving more time to concentrate upon other more time-demanding issues, such as keeping the promotional pressure up on the touring front:

SR: We don't leave the venues to their own resources . . . we check the ticket sales and work them.

ER: That's how it built, she would sell out so quickly, people would say is she doing another night, well, no! So we need a bigger venue . . . and that's how it grows . . . but we do always keep them aware of the show, we work at it all the time.

SR: We had gigs early on where they'd book her and then we realised they weren't selling tickets, just first come first served, and it was a nightmare . . . we'd have people there really angry, they'd driven from here and there, queuing round the block.

ER: That's when we put the disclaimer on the website about checking before you travel.

These examples of how Pure came to formulate its methodologies and business models are all, we note, entirely empirical, and it is perhaps in this aspect that its success as a business lies. Yet of course no amount of financial smarts are going to save you if the product is of little or no interest to people.

While Kate Rusby has produced recent albums either by herself or with her brother, Joe Rusby's role in his sister's success can hardly be overstated; his adroit, innate and inherently musical productions on the albums and his skill as a sound engineer in the live environment are central to her past and enduring success as a recording artist and live draw. The in-house studio is all part of this and Pure's for-hire PA was used for early tours but now bigger equipment tends to be brought in for the larger venues.

AR: Joe ended up having to hire in more and more gear to the point where it wasn't worth it, so we just hire it all now. Joe is really talented as a soundman. He was a chorister and has a fantastic ear for sounds, so he has been a big part of Kate's sound recorded and live. Having the studio in the house is fantastic for Kate, so she can come and go, come back tomorrow if it's not working today, no pressure, just make it right and that feeling comes across on the records I think . . . it's your own space.

So, to restate, the Pure set-up functions entirely in-house – publicity, promotion, finance, agent, promoter, sound equipment, live production, studio production – each family member having their own very important role in the operation as a whole. To have a set-up like this may not be entirely unique, but for it to be in the service of such a successful act and to have not been compromised by that success is remarkable indeed. Finally, I wondered what, aside from this careful attention to business and detail of packaging, production and presentation, had made this new operation so wildly successful:

AR: What it was was Kate! That made the difference. Plus of course she's been backed by some superb musicians, including her ex-husband John McCusker, who was absolutely fanatical about detail, quite brilliant, and did a lot of the musical arrangements. He also brought his expertise and knowledge of the folk scene to us and other musicians that he knew to Kate's music. He was very outgoing, always talking to people, so he'd get to know people so when her first album came out, he'd go to people and say 'listen to this', and the musicians he knew have always been the best. People have often said, 'why don't you do something different Kate, why don't you put these pop songs on your album or go out and find some contemporary material or covers?' but she'll say well this is what I do!

ER: Kate feels lucky . . . she didn't plan any of this along the way, although Dad did of course . . . when we had the *My Music* show [a 60-minute documentary for Channel 5 in 2008], she came across really well . . . doing the ironing backstage . . . that's her, what she does!

AR: So in the end it's purely Kate . . . not only the music, which speaks for itself, but also her rapport with the audience is important . . . some felt she talks too much onstage, and wanted her to shut up and sing, but that's what made the connection . . .

PM: And that's something from the folk club that has survived the transition, holding those two worlds together, isn't it?

SR: Yes, that's it, she's always told the tale, always told the tale.

So if part of the appeal of Kate Rusby's work on record and on stage is that it strongly resounds with tradition – the found, learned and shared repertoire, the first-rate musicians that always surround her, the stagecraft of the folk club surviving into the big halls – these elements of music and performance also clearly and firmly innovate around such tradition. This also goes for the way her parent company does business. Pure is the exception that proves the rule: a hugely successful enterprise which rests not only on the output of one person, but which provides a platform for a carefully selected roster – just like any other record label – yet one which is entirely independent and uniquely managed. Many labels may claim to be 'like a family' but Pure can rely on the strengths as well as the tensions of such a situation. Ironically, when we have spoken such a lot about tradition, it was the decision to not organise itself like a 'traditional' record company that made the difference for Pure, and it arguably provides an innovative model for the independent sector to follow in the present troubled period for the music industry. In its own quiet way Pure is possibly the most radical independent musical enterprise currently working in the UK.

Indie labels

1. What advantages does an independent label have over a corporate or 'major' one?
2. What are the disadvantages of running such a label as opposed to working within a larger and more corporate set-up?
3. Are indie labels 'in business' just as fully as the largest major or is such a label in pursuit of some other goal?
4. Find out about independent labels in your area – how 'indie' are they? Are they allied to a recording studio? Are they related to or dependent upon the local scene, clubs or shops or do they draw acts in from a larger area?

Conclusion

In this difficult time for the music industry, when all the rules according to which the game has been run for decades seem to be simply melting away, there are a number of ways the industry can look forward and ensure its survival. Our studies of the business and ethical models of the independent label have investigated what these new conditions might look like. The wider industries of mediation that run parallel to and attend upon the music such as the press, television and radio are all encountering similar disruptions as the digital and new media platforms assert themselves and seem to make the long-standing models look redundant. As the rules of the game change, those who seek to mediate the music will need to take notice of the new ways it is being made and, far more than was once the case, to be attentive to the way that music is being produced, sold and, finally, seen and heard. This is the central point of music, now as it ever was.

Appendix I: 'Hail, Hail, Rock'n'Roll' column by Laura Barton, *The Guardian*, Friday, 11 April 2008

Introduction

I've been writing 'Hail, Hail, Rock'n'Roll' for over four and a half years now, so this column about a concert at the Church of St Barnabas appeared fairly early in its lifetime. But it has amused me to read it again this week – only yesterday I filed my latest column, and it was about the relationship between preachers in the black church and soul music – Solomon Burke, Otis Redding, Sam Cooke. The columns are quite an eclectic bunch. I'm not tethered to writing about new artists or big events, and this grants me a lot of freedom. I can write about moments like this – church shows, hymns, Neil Young records, a throwaway pop hit, and the next week write about something wildly different – the joys of dancing, road trips, an art show. I think it works because this is how we all actually listen to music; we don't all spend the week listening to the latest releases, rather we find that we wake up with a fierce desire to listen to Tina Turner or the Monkees, set shuffle on our iPods and suddenly we're seven years old again and dancing round the living room with our brothers. So that's all the column is, really; even if you don't know or don't like the music I'm writing about, I hope that at least you might recognise the sensation of it.

Laura Barton, July 2011

The Chapel of St Barnabas sits on Manette Street, between the scuffle of Charing Cross Road and the bluster of Greek Street, at the very edge of Soho. Past the Borderline, before the Pillars of Hercules, a nondescript metal gate leads to a low, huddled doorway and on through a dim passage to the chapel itself, where stands an altar with soft red marble pillars. From time to time, musical performances are held here, before the rows of chairs set out in lieu of pews, in the space beneath the blue semi-dome painted with golden stars, in a small, calm clearing that somehow makes me think of that Lorca line: 'The still pool of your mouth, under a thicket of kisses.'

A little while ago, I was here at St Barnabas for a showcase held by XL Recordings: there were videos from the Raconteurs and Vampire Weekend, Phill Jupitus played jovial host, and the evening culminated in a live performance by Cajun Dance Party. I have, it occurred to me midway through the evening, probably been to more gigs in churches than I have religious services. From a bill featuring Belle and Sebastian and Arab Strap, to a more recent line-up of Emmy the Great, the Mountain Goats and Micah P. Hinson at the Union Chapel in London. And they always enrapture me. I remember going by myself to see Sigur Rós play such a gig one early summer evening, many years ago. The air was still warm, you could hear birdsong drifting through the open chapel door, and as they played, I remember a feeling more transcendent, more glad-hearted than I had experienced at any harvest festival or carol service. It appeared to me then, as it appears to me now, that it does not matter whether it is 'Silent Night' or 'Svefn-g-englar' that fills those church walls; the thing about music in churches is that its performance feels like a celebration of creation, an affirmation of how damned glorious it is to be alive. As Stravinsky put it: 'The Church knew what the psalmist knew: Music praises God. Music is well or better able to praise him than the building of the church and all its decoration; it is the Church's greatest ornament.'

What I like about churches is somehow what I also like about musical instruments and lyrics and songs – that they only truly come alive with human contact. Cold marble, hard pews, stained glass, share much with guitar strings, piano keys, CDs, sentences, syllables, that in their inhabitation, in their playing there comes the sense of the inanimate made flesh. To hear the heave and huff of the church organ, to hear the swell of the choir and the congregation, to feel music and voices rising to the rafters, is to see life breathed into the building itself. And so to hear Jonathan Richman at the Union Chapel, or Patti Smith incanting at St Giles, or even 'All Things Bright and Beautiful' sung with glory and gusto in a small Lancashire church, brings to me a similar shiver as that first snap and crackle as needle kisses vinyl; the sense that something has been resuscitated.

There was a television series first screened in the mid-1970s, named *A Passion for Churches*, which saw John Betjeman waxing lyrical about the churches of Britain. I've only ever seen it on YouTube, but in the clip I like to watch when I'm far from home or sick of the city, he is rhapsodising about Norfolk churches. There are shots of Wymondham Abbey, the rich green of the churchyard, and stained glass windows showing bewinged and halo-ed angels engaged in silent, motionless musical pursuit: lute, violin and horn; cymbal, trumpet, tambourine and triangle. And then in the final moment comes a clutch of pale-skinned, blue-clad choirboys rehearsing 'Ye Holy Angels Bright'. 'Behold! Behold! Behold!' they sing, as the choirmaster tuts, and the piano wheezes, breathing life, suddenly, into their stained-glass friends. And above it all, in its well-articulated chug, rises the voice of Betjeman himself, reading a line from Psalm 150:6: 'Let everything that has breath praise the Lord.'

Appendix II: Content Analysis of Issue of *Music Week*, 18 September 2010

This seems a fairly representative issue, with its mix of the routine and the extraordinary. The business always seems to be on the threshold of another 'important phase' and that's here for all to see. Looking back just this short distance you can see how fast things move – some campaigns work, some don't, and that's because the most important thing is, after all, the music and that can't be quantified, thank goodness.

Paul Williams, editor, *Music Week*, February 2011

The magazine's masthead at the top of the first page is 'Music Week' and 'The Business of Music', with the date '18.09.10'. Unlike the consumer monthlies which specify month, year and issue number we see here a difference in turnover and purpose – the business changes week on week. The magazine comes in a 'wraparound' cover, featuring advertising content in this issue it is, somewhat bizarrely, 'The Modkatz', an animated band featuring cats dressed as Mods. This kind of act/product would never get a sniff of a front cover in the consumer press yet in *Music Week*, which sells advertising space on its front and back covers, the project gets potentially valuable exposure to the dealers and stockists. In this we can see immediately that the paper is faithful to its strapline, 'The Business of Music'. In this the magazine is also shown to employ different criteria to the consumer monthlies, where covers are 'earned', 'awarded' and 'prestigious' – although, of course, they are in their own way just as business driven. However, the selling of the front and back covers gets round the 'newspaper' problem – a text-heavy front page becomes a striking image.

Inside, page 3 of the magazine is actually page 1 – and the pagination starts from here, so that the inside back cover, despite carrying key chart information, has no 'official' page number. The masthead information is reproduced just as it is on the sponsored front page, and beneath it are three spots trailing content inside, one headed 'News' (a piece on sales of the album by Manchester band Hurts) and two 'Features', one spotlighting Tinie Tempah and a big piece on the 'Fourth Quarter', the most important period for music retailers, between September and Christmas – traditionally the busiest time for key releases in the year. Below these trails, and where a consumer monthly would be bedecked in eye-catching photographs and names, *Music Week* gets straight to business with a detailed piece by editor Paul Williams on the future plans of the EMI group for artist development. It also relates to a large chunk of the 'advertorial' on the autumn's release schedule inside. The lower part of the page considers the sales potential of a Mercury prize win for band The xx, and, tellingly, focuses not on the musical content, but the way this win is to be used in the subsequent re-promotion of the album.

Page 2 features, as do the consumer magazines, a 'Playlist' of what the writers are listening to, or what is new and being currently vigorously promoted. 'Gig of the Week' is also an index of where the promotional budget is going, the nominated show being new band 'Everything Everything's album launch at fashionable XOYO in London. They are promoted as 'indie' despite being signed to Geffen. The promo gig is later to be cancelled at short notice. The news page also trails the 'Q4' feature by talking up the retail possibilities of the period between September and Christmas – placing particular emphasis on the planned Take That album with Robbie Williams, a new Kings of Leon LP and Cheryl Cole's second album. An equally sized piece features the proposed retail/sales conferences in the same period. The facing page carries a piece building on the front page's segment on The xx, and details personnel moves within the business, with Mercury Records general manager in the UK being reported as having moved to a similar role at Polydor. Far right of page 3, we find the contents column for the magazine.

Page 4 is headed 'News' and features an erudite editorial from Paul Williams on the varying fortunes of EMI in the past few years. The consensus seems to be that if EMI fails, the entire industry catches a cold. This is an intriguing dichotomy in a fiercely competitive industry. A reader's poll question bottoms out the page. Other news stories are a small features on The Modkatz (the featured act on the wraparound cover), the Hurts, and a call from the Musician's Union to the Con-Dem coalition to reconsider cuts to the Department of Culture, Media and Sport.

Pages 6/7 are headed 'news media' featuring analysis and statistics on TV, radio and pre-release airplay, alongside short pieces on radio campaigns for albums by Brandon Flowers of the Killers and rapper Usher. There is also a longer more speculative piece on the rapidly growing and diverging number of media platforms for promotion, focusing particularly on microsites on radio station websites.

Page 8 is headed 'News Live' and discusses cases of alleged prejudice against 'urban' music events by Manchester City Council and the upcoming 'Turning Point' festival at London's Roundhouse. There are charts here too, for Live Events – where box office gross is the index of success. Aerosmith's show at the O2 smashes all comers this particular week. Also quantified are 'Primary Ticketing' (that is, first sales of tickets for any given event) and, somewhat incredibly, 'Ticket Resale Price Chart' which shows what the current resale value (i.e. above and beyond face value) of tickets for future events is each week, compiled via the Tixdaq website.

Page 10 is 'News Digital', given over to the online relaunch of 4AD, the label devised by Ivo Watts-Russell which brought us Cocteau Twins, This Mortal Coil, Heidi Berry and the Les Mystère des Voix Bulgares albums. Small news 'cuts' detail, among other matters, Eminem's dispute with Universal over digital rights and the usefulness of social networking sites to music promotion. Page 11 is headed 'News Publishing', detailing the revival of contemporary folk/world label Cooking Vinyl's publishing operation, EMI's plan to develop its publishing concerns in the continental European markets and the first 'SongFest' songwriting workshop in October 2010, featuring tuition sessions given by Newton Faulkner. The final news page is a 'Diary', gathering in material and snippets of news which don't quite fit into the other categories, presented in a more chatty and humorous style. It also gives a plug to a new act in the 'Unearthed' spot, in this case Island Records' new signing Lauren Pritchard.

Page 13 carries the first feature, a piece profiling EMI act Tinie Tempah. The tone of the piece is not wildly unlike what we might read in the daily newspaper pop columns or even in the genre-specific music monthly, but tellingly emphasises names and numbers of producers, record labels and promotional campaigners. On page 15, the big feature opens – headed 'The Q Factor' the bulk of the magazine's editorial content concerns itself with the all-important 'Fourth Quarter' or 'Q4'. This blends editorial with contextualised advertising – remember this is a trade publication, so the lines between criticism and promotion, often blurred and slyly fudged in the consumer magazines, is more clearly demarcated in *Music Week* – it's all about selling, with notions of aesthetic judgement further down the agenda. So we have three pages of text about the possible impact of the Q4, the sales and promotional value of guest slots on the X Factor, and the view of the major retailers, particularly HMV – the retail arm of EMI, of course. The tone is upbeat – as it is throughout the magazine – closing with a quote from Melanie Armstrong of HMV's 'Head of Music and Impulse': 'It's all great for Christmas. The line up for Q4 is looking really exciting.'

Pages 18–27 lay out in generous spatial and approving terms just how 'exciting' this period might be for retailers, listing planned releases by label/music group – the order is EMI, Sony, Universal with a double-page spread each, followed by highlights from the proposed release schedules of Atlantic, Warner Bros, Rhino and Absolute. It is interesting that despite three of these labels being owned by Universal they are listed separately, as the label names carry great cultural value and cachet in the field of popular music history. They are in themselves very strong brands and are worth promoting and protecting by the corporate owner.

Pages 30–2 list 'Key Releases', not just of the issue's week but right up to, as it says, 'November 8 and beyond', deep into the critical 'Q4' for the retailers. These pages also contain, in the grand tradition of the music weekly, Single and Album of the Week, 'Last Ones Standing' by Example and 'Science and Faith' by The Script respectively, both given very short but very positive reviews. There is also 'The Panel', where four singles are, again, given uniformly positive write-ups by an anonymous panel of 'specialist media tastemakers'. 'Catalogue Reviews' quickly detail a quartet of more obscure releases/reissues to acknowledge the growing awareness that the record retailer depends more and more upon customers of a certain age who acquired the record buying habit in the period 1960–90 and have not altogether abandoned the traditional record shop.

This page also begins the Chart segment of the magazine – this is in some way *Music Week*'s most famous and certainly most widely seen section – how many record retailers in the 1970s and 190s posted the old format 'centrefold' of the top 50 in their shop somewhere? Amazingly, this issue of *Music Week* offers twenty-three different charts – that's just shy of two dozen ways of measuring the momentary success of a piece of music, an album of songs or matters arising from both or either.

The charts included in the 18 September 2010 issue of *Music Week* were:

The Official UK Singles Chart (Top 75)
The Official UK Albums Chart (Top 75)
Indie Singles (Top 20)
Indie Albums (Top 20)

Indie Albums Breakers (Top 10)
Compilation Chart (Top 10)
Classical Albums (Top 10)
TV Airplay Chart (Top 40)
UK Radio Airplay Chart (Top 50)
Pre-Release Singles Radio Play (Top 20)
Pre-Release Album Radio Play Chart (Top 20)
Dance Albums (Top 10)
Online 'Buzz' Chart (Top 20)
Amazon Pre-Release Chart (Top 20)
HMV Pre-Release Chart (Top 20)
Shazam Pre-Release Chart (Top 20)
Catalogue Greatest Hits (Top 20)
Box Score Live Events Chart (Top 10)
Hitwise Primary Ticketing Chart (Top 20)
Tixdaq Ticket Resale Price Chart (Top 20)

Club Charts:
Upfront Club (Top 40)
Commercial Pop (Top 30)
Urban (Top 30)
Cool Cuts (Top 20)

The main UK single and album charts give the current position, last week's position and the number of weeks on the chart. Also included are publishing, composition, production and record label details alongside catalogue numbers, so that there might be no mistakes in ordering exact titles or even versions of titles. Here, in full, is the 'stock market for your hi-fi' as described by The Rezillos on their 1978 hit 'Top of the Pops', who's in, who's out, who's going up, who's coming down, where to place your bets. *Music Week* foregrounds this process and with commendable directness reveals that the music industry is just that – an industry, trying to find a product that the potential audience will be prepared to invest in long term, so that EMI or Universal will be able to recoup their own investments. Consequently, and perhaps unexpectedly, *Music Week* is probably the most honest music publication available on the magazine shelves.

Appendix III: *Down in the Grooves* playlist, 10 October 2009

The playlist encapsulates what I do – a mix of records I've had for years, things I've recently bought plus the odd thing sent to me by record companies. Genre-wise there's blues, soul, 60s garage punk, dancefloor jazz, afro funk, Ethiopian jazz, fuzzy heavy rock, Hammond workouts, music library stuff, folk, psychedelia and loads more.

The ethos is that if you don't like a particular track or genre, you won't have to wait long before something else comes along. I tend to play two tracks together if they're from the same genre or if there's a connection – both covers of a certain artist for example. I tend not to have too much structure as I believe that if soul fans thought I only played soul tunes in the first hour they might not listen for the whole programme.

James Addyman, presenter/producer, *Down in the Grooves*, BBC Radio Leeds, June 2011

Playlist for show dated 10 October 2009:

Gray's Bounce – Henry Gray (Excello)
I Got to Get to California – Marvin Gaye (Tamla Motown)
I Gotta Get Away (From My Own Self) – Millie Jackson (Southbound)
Hydrogen Atom – The Bedlam Four (Armada)
My Baby Don't Care – The Gants (Liberty)
Hairy Mary – Big Boss Man (Blow Up)
Mo'Reen – Danny & Jerry (Ronn)
Incantations – Afro Blues Quintet Plus One (Mira)
The Turnaround (Pt 1) – Hank Mobley (Blue Note)
Psych-out Sanctorum – The Storybook (Sidewalk)
It's Been Too Long – Quicksilver Messenger Service (Capitol)
Gedamay – Getatchew Mekurya (L'Arome)
Feeling You Got – El Rego Et Ses Commandos (Analog Africa)
Love Potion No. 9 – Jewel Akens (Era)

Shake Around – Ray Smith (Charly)
Living – Alice Cooper (Straight)
The Dog, the Dog, He's at It Again – Caravan (Deram)
Poseidon – Franco Tamponi (Irma)
Get Out of My Life Woman – George Semper (Imperial)
Raindreams – The Lords (Columbia)
Hanky Panky–- The Outsiders (Capitol)
It's Alright by Me – The Magic Mixture (Saga)
(I Can't Get No) Satisfaction – Blue Cheer (Philips)
Let It Out – J. J. Jackson (Strike)
Little Darling – The Flirtations (Deram)
I Can't Keep from Crying Sometimes – Davy Graham (Decca)
Babe in Arms – Buffy Sainte-Marie (Vanguard)
Just Can't Stay – Willie Nix (Sabre)
So Called Friend – Billy Lamont (Bran-T)
Get Right – The Players (Minit)
21st Century Kenya – The Electrostats (Three Oaks)
As Jesus Wore His Own – Los Vidrios Quebrados (UES)
No Place or Time – The Echoes Of Carnaby Street (Thames)
The Law – Andy Capp (Trojan)
All in One – The Valentines (Attack)

Discography

Andersson, Benny, *Benny Andersson's Orkester* (Mono Music 2001)

Babylon Zoo, 'Spaceman', *Boy with the X-Ray Eyes* (EMI 1996)

Bunyan, Vashti, *Another Diamond Day* (Philips 1970)

Dandy Warhols, 'Bohemian Like You', *Thirteen Tales from Urban Bohemia* (Chrysalis 2000)

Drake, Nick:
- 'Pink Moon', *Pink Moon* (Island 1972)
- 'Hanging on a Star', *Time of No Reply* (Hannibal 1986)

Drever, Kris, *Black Water* (Navigator 2006)

Everything but the Girl:
- 'Night and Day' EP (Cherry Red 1984)
- 'Missing' (Virgin 1995)
- *Eden* (Blanco y Negro 1984)
- *Amplified Heart* (Virgin 1994)
- *Walking Wounded* (Virgin 1996)
- *Temperamental* (Virgin 1999)

Gang of Four, 'Natural's Not in It', *Entertainment!* (EMI 1979)

Gonzales, Jose, 'Heartbeats', *Veneer* (Imperial Stockholm 2003)

Half Man Half Biscuit, *Back In The DHSS* (Probe Plus 1985)

Henriksen, Arve, *Cartography* (ECM 2008)

Kraftwerk, 'Musique Non Stop', *Electric Cafe* (KlingKlang/EMI 1986)

Le Mystère des Voix Bulgares (Disques Cellier 1975; issued in UK 1988 by 4AD)

Leftfield, 'Phat Planet', *Rhythm and Stealth* (Chrysalis 1999)

Massive Attack, *Protection* (Virgin 1994)

Proclaimers, *The Best of . . .* (Persevere Records 2002)

Radiohead, *In Rainbows* (download only 2007; subsequently on CD via XL)

Rezillos, The, 'Top of the Pops', *Can't Stand the Rezillos* (Sire 1978)

Rodamaal, 'Love Island', 'Musica Feliz' (Buzzin' Fly 2003)

Rusby, Kate:
- *Kate Rusby and Kathryn Roberts* (Pure 1995)
- *Hourglass* (1998)
- *Sleepless* (1999)
- *Little Lights* (2001)

- *10* (2002)
- *Underneath the Stars* (2004)
- *The Girl Who Couldn't Fly* (2005)
- *Awkward Annie* (2007)
- *Sweet Bells* (2008)
- *Make the Light* (2010)
- *While Mortals Sleep* (2011)

Sex Pistols, 'God Save the Queen', *Never Mind the Bollocks Here's the Sex Pistols* (Virgin 1977)

Siberry, Jane:
- *Dragon Dreams* (IssaLight 2008)
- *With What Shall I Keep Warm?* (IssaLight 2009)

Slettahjell, Solveig, *Antologie* (Universal 2011)

Sports, The, 'Who Listens To The Radio?' (EP Stiff Records 1979)

Stiltskin, 'Inside', *The Mind's Eye* (EastWest 1994)

Watt, Ben, 'Lone Cat' (Buzzin' Fly 2003)

Various artists, *Pillows and Prayers* (Cherry Red 1983)

Links

Buzzin' Fly: http://www.buzzinfly.com/
Down in the Grooves: http://www.bbc.co.uk/news/uk-england-leeds-12959193
'Hail Hail Rock'n'Roll': http://www.guardian.co.uk/music/series/hailhail
   rocknroll
Jane Siberry: http://www.janesiberry.com/home/music.html
John Lennon Citroën ad: http://www.youtube.com/watch?v=4Ph4rZU0Ns4
Late Junction: http://www.bbc.co.uk/programmes/b006tp52
Later . . . With Jools Holland: http://www.bbc.co.uk/later/
Music Week: http://www.musicweek.com/
'One Laptop per Child' campaign: http://www.youtube.com/
   watch?v=Oz9R82vWw08
Pure Records: http://www.purerecords.net/
Songlines magazine: http://www.songlines.co.uk/
Word magazine: http://www.wordmagazine.co.uk/

Bibliography

Austerlitz, Saul (2008) *Money for Nothing: A History of the Music Video from the Beatles to the White Stripes*. New York: Continuum.

Becker, Howard S. (1992) *Art Worlds*. San Francisco: University of California Press.

Bangs, Lester (2001) *Psychotic Reactions and Carburetor Dung*. London: Serpent's Tail.

Bennett, A. (2000) *Popular Music and Youth Culture: Music, Identity and Place*. London: Palgrave.

Bennett, A. (2001) *Cultures of Popular Music*. Milton Keynes: Open University Press.

Bohlma, P. (2002) *World Music: A Very Short Introduction*. London: Oxford University Press.

Bourdieu, Pierre (1987) *Distinction: A Social Critique of the Judgement of Taste*. London: Routledge.

Boyd, Joe (2006) *White Bicycles: Making Music in the 1960s*. London: Serpent's Tail.

Bradshaw, Ben (2009) 'Music and digital futures', *Music Week*, 10 September.

Brocken, Michael (2003) *The British Folk Revival 1944–2002*. Aldershot: Ashgate.

Broughton, Simon (ed.) (1993) *The Rough Guide to World Music*, 2 vols: Vol. 1: *Africa and the Middle East*; Vol. 2: *Europe and Asia*. London: Penguin/Rough Guides; see also 2009 edition.

Broughton, Simon (196) Letter to *Gramophone*, July, p. 8.

Carpenter, Humphrey (1996) *The Envy of the World: Fifty years of the BBC Third Programme and Radio 3, 1946–1996*. London: Weidenfeld & Nicolson.

Chalmers, K. (2008) *Béla Bartók*. London: Phaidon.

Clayton, Herbert Middleton (eds) (2003) *The Cultural Study of Music*. London: Routledge.

Cohen, Stanley (1966) *Folk Devils and Moral Panics*. London: McGibbon & Kee.

Conway, Steve (2009) *ShipRocked: Life on the Waves with Radio Caroline*. London: Liberties Press.

Dennen, Frederic (1991) *Hit Men: Power Brokers and Fast Money Inside the Music Business*. New York: Vintage.

Eagleton, Terry (1964) 'New bearings: The Beatles', *Blackfriars* [journal], 45: 175–8.

Elmes, Simon (2008) *And Now on Radio 4: A Celebration of the World's Best Radio Station*. London: Arrow.

Fletcher, Winston (2008) *Powers of Persuasion: The Inside Story of British Advertising 1951–2000*. Oxford: Oxford University Press.

Ford, Simon (1999) *Wreckers of Civilisation: The Story of Coum Transmissions and Throbbing Gristle*. London: Black Dog.

Forster, E. M. [1927] (2009) *Aspects of the Novel*. London: Penguin.

Frith, Simon and Goodwin, A. (eds) (1990) *On Record: Rock Pop and the Written Word*. London: Routledge.

Frith, Simon and Goodwin, Andrew (1994) *Sound and Vision: A Music Video Reader*. London: Faber.

Frith, Simon (1978) *The Sociology of Rock*. London: Constable.

Frith, Simon (1988) *Music for Pleasure*. London: Polity Press.

Frith, Simon (1998) *Performing Rites: On the Value of Popular Music*. Oxford: Oxford University Press.

Garfield, Simon (1999) *The Nation's Favourite: The True Adventures of Radio 1*. London: Faber.

Goodman, Fred (1998) *The Mansion on the Hill: Dylan, Young, Geffen, Springsteen, and the Head-on Collision of Rock and Commerce*. New York: Vintage.

Goodwin, Andrew (1993) *Dancing in the Distraction Factory*. London: Faber.

Gorman, Paul (2001) *In Their Own Write: Adventures in the Music Press*. London: Sanctuary.

Gray, Louise (2009) *No-Nonsense Guide to World Music*. London: New Internationalist.

Gronow, Pekka and Saunio, Ilpo (1999) *An International History of the Recording Industry*. London: Cassell.

Grossberg, L. (1992) *We Gotta Get Out of This Place*. London: Routledge.

Guralnick, Peter (1998) *Searching for Robert Johnson: The Life and Legend of the 'King of the Delta Blues Singers'*. London: Plume Books.

Harris, Bob (2001) *The Whispering Years*. London: BBC Books.

Hays, Constance L. (2007) *Pop: Truth and Power at the Coca-Cola Company*. New York: Arrow Books.

Hebdige, Dick (1979) *Subcultures: The Meaning of Style*. Milton Keynes: Open University Press.

Hendy, David (2007) *Life on Air: A History of Radio Four*. London: Oxford University Press.

Hesmondhalgh, D. (ed.) (2002) *Popular Music Studies*. London: Bloomsbury.

Hesmondalgh, D. (2004) *The Cultural Industries*. London: Sage.

Hoggart, Richard (1957) *The Uses of Literacy: Aspects of Working Class Life*. London: Chatto & Windus.

Hooley, Terri (2010) *Hooleygan: Music, Mayhem, Good Vibrations*. Belfast: Blackstaff Press.

Hoover, Michael and Stokes, Lisa (1998) 'Gang of Four shrinkwraps entertainment', *Popular Music and Society*, 22 (3): 21–38.

Inglis, Ian (2003) *Popular Music and Film*. London: Wallflower Press.

Inglis, Ian (2006) *The Performance of Popular Music: History, Place and Time*. Aldershot: Ashgate.

Inglis, Ian (2010) *Popular Music and Television in Britain*. Aldershot: Ashgate.

Johns, Adrian (2010) *Death of a Pirate: British Radio and the Making of the Information Age*. London: W. W. Norton.

Jones, C. W. (2008) *The Rock Canon: Canonical Values in the Reception of Rock Albums*. Aldershot: Ashgate.

Jones, Graham (2010) *Last Shop Standing: Whatever Happened to Record Shops?* London: Proper.

Jones, Steve (ed.) (2002) *Pop Music and the Press*. Philadelphia: Temple University Press.

Kershaw, A. (2011) *No Off Switch*. London: Serpent's Tail

King, Mike (2009) *Music Marketing: Press, Promotion, Distribution, and Retail*. Boston: Berklee Press.

Klein, Bethany (2010) *As Heard on TV: Popular Music in Advertising*. Aldershot: Ashgate.

Knopper, Steve (2009) *Appetite for Self-destruction: The Spectacular Crash of the Record Industry in the Digital Age*. London: Simon & Schuster.

Kusek, David and Gerd, Leonard (2005) *The Future of Music: Manifesto for the Digital Music Revolution*. London: Omnibus Press.

Lazell, Barry (2000) *Indie Hits: The Complete UK Singles and Album Independent Charts, 1980–89*. London: Cherry Red Books.

Leppert, R. (ed.) (2002) *Adorno: Essays on Music*. San Francisco: University of California Press.

Lester, Paul (2008) *Damaged Gods: Gang of Four*. London: Omnibus.

Link, N. (2009) *Kicking Up a Racket: The Story of Stiff Little Fingers 1977–1983*. Belfast: Appletree Press.

Lomax, Alan (1993) *The Land Where the Blues Began*. New York: Pantheon.

Macdonald, Ian (1994) *Revolution in the Head: The Beatles' Records and the Sixties*. London: Fourth Estate.

Marcus, Greil (1972) *Mystery Train*. London: Penguin.

Middleton, Richard (1972) *Pop Music and the Blues: A Study of the Relationship and Its Significance*. London: Gollancz.

Middleton, Richard (1990) *Studying Popular Music*. Philadelphia: Open University Press.

Middleton, Richard (2006) *Voicing the Popular: On the Subjects of Popular Music*. London: Routledge.

Middleton, Richard, Clayton, Martin and Herbert, Trevor (eds) (2003) *The Cultural Study of Music: A Critical Introduction*. London: Routledge.

Mills, Peter (2010) *Hymns to the Silence: Inside the Words and Music of Van Morrison*. New York: Continuum.

Mills, Peter (2010) 'Stone Fox Chase: *The Old Grey Whistle Test* and the rise of high pop television', in Ian Inglis (ed.), *Popular Music and Television in Britain*. Aldershot: Ashgate.

Mills, Peter (1994) 'Gang of Four', in Mark Ellingham (ed.), *The Rough Guide to Rock*. London: Penguin Rough Guides.

Moore, Allan (ed.) (2009) *Analyzing Popular Music*. Cambridge: Cambridge University Press.

Muggleton, David (2000) *Inside Subculture: The Post-Modern Meaning of Style*. London: Berg.

Muggleton, David and Weinzerl, Rupert (eds) (2003) *The Post-Subcultures Reader*. London: Berg.

Mundy, John (1999) *Popular Music on Screen*. Manchester: Manchester University Press.

Negus, Keith (1996) *Popular Music in Theory: An Introduction*. London: Polity.

Negus, Keith (1999) *Music Genres and Corporate Cultures*. London: Routledge.

Nice, James (2011) *Shadowplayers: The Rise and Fall of Factory Records*. London: Aurum Press.

Nidel, Richard O. (2004) *World Music: The Basics*. London: Routledge.

Nightingale, Annie (2000) *Wicked Speed*. London: Pan Books.

O'Neill, Sean (2003) *It Makes You Want to Spit: The Definitive Guide to Punk in Northern Ireland*. Belfast: Reekus.

Osborne, John (2010) *Radio Head: Up and Down the Dial of British Radio*. London: Pocket Books.

Peel, John (2006) *Margrave of the Marshes*. London: Corgi.

Pendergrast, Mark (2000) *For God, Country, and Coca-Cola: The Definitive History of the Great American Soft Drink and the Company That Makes It*. London: Basic Books.

Petrusich, Amanda (2007) *Pink Moon*. New York: Continuum.

Pettit, Emma (2008) *Old Rare New: The Independent Record Shop*. New York: Black Dog.

Railton, D. and Watson, P. (2011) *Music Video and the Politics of Representation*. Edinburgh: Edinburgh University Press.

Ritz, David (2005) *Divided Soul: The Life of Marvin Gaye*, revised 3rd edn. London: Omnibus.

Reising, Russell (ed.) (2002) *Every Sound There Is: The Beatles' Revolver and the Transformation of Rock and Roll*. Aldershot: Ashgate.

Reising, Russell (ed.) (2006) *Speak To Me: The Legacy of Pink Floyd's Dark Side of the Moon*. Aldershot: Ashgate.

Said, Edward (1978) *Orientalism*. London: Penguin.

Sandoval, Andrew (2006) *The Monkees: Day by Day Story of the 60s Pop Sensation*. London: Jawbone.

Schwartz, Daylle Deana (2009) *Start and Run Your Own Record Label*. New York: Billboard Books.

Shelton, Robert [1986] (2011) *No Direction Home: The Life and Music of Bob Dylan*. London: Omnibus.

Shuker, Roy (2005) *Popular Music: The Key Concepts*. London: Routledge.

Shuker, Roy (2007) *Understanding Popular Music Culture*. London: Routledge.

Stoller, David (2010) *Sounds of Your Life: A History of Independent Radio in the UK*. London: John Libbey.

Sweers, Britta (2005) *Electric Folk: The Changing Face of English Traditional Music*. New York: Oxford University Press.

Taylor, N. (2010) *Document and Eyewitness: An Intimate History of Rough Trade: The Rough Trade Story*. London: Orion.

Thornton, Sarah (1995) *Club Cultures: Music, Media and Subcultural Capital*. London: Polity.

Tungate, Mark (2007) *Ad Land: A Global History of Advertising*. London: Kogan Page.

Wald, Elijah (2005) *Escaping the Delta: Robert Johnson and the Invention of the Blues*. London: HarperCollins.

Watt, Ben (1997) *Patient: The True Story of a Rare Illness*. London: Penguin

Wernick, Andrew (1991) *Promotional Culture*. London: Sage.

Whiteley, Sheila (1993) *The Space Between the Notes*. London: Routledge.

Whiteley, Sheila (1997) *Sexing the Groove*. London: Routledge.

Whiteley, Sheila (2000) *Women and Popular Music: Sexuality, Identity and Subjectivity*. London: Routledge.

Whiteley, Sheila (2005) *Too Much Too Young*. London: Routledge.

Wilson, Tony and Robertson, Matthew (2007) *Factory Records: The Complete Graphic Album*. London: Thames & Hudson.

Young, R. (2010) *Electric Eden*. London: Faber.

Index